AFRICAN AMERICAN CHRONOLOGY

AFRICAN AMERICAN REFERENCE LIBRARY

AFRICAN AMERICAN CHRONOLOGY

VOLUME 2
1973-1993

by Alton Hornsby, Jr. and Deborah Gillan Straub

An Imprint of Gale Research Inc.

AFRICAN AMERICAN CHRONOLOGY

Alton Hornsby, Jr., and Deborah Gillan Straub, Editors

STAFF

Carol DeKane Nagel, *U·X·L Developmental Editor*
Thomas L. Romig, *U·X·L Publisher*

Amy Marcaccio, *Acquisitions Editor*

Shanna P. Heilveil, *Production Assistant*
Evi Seoud, *Assistant Production Manager*
Mary Beth Trimper, *Production Director*

Cynthia Baldwin, *Art Director*
Arthur Chartow, *Technical Design Services Manager*

Weigl Educational Publishers Limited, *Page and Cover Design and Typesetting*

This book is printed on acid-free paper that meets the minimum requirements of American National Standard for Information Sciences—Permanence Paper for Printed Library Materials, ANSI Z39.48-1984.

ISBN 0-8103-9231-3 (Set)
ISBN 0-8103-9233-X (Volume 2)

Printed in the United States of America

Published simultaneously in the United Kingdom
by Gale Research International Limited
(An affiliated company of Gale Research Inc.)

The trademark **ITP** is used under license.

AFRICAN AMERICAN REFERENCE LIBRARY

ADVISORY BOARD

AFRICAN AMERICAN REFERENCE LIBRARY

The **African American Reference Library** fills the need for a comprehensive, curriculum-related reference covering all aspects of African American life and culture. Aimed primarily at middle school and junior high school students, this nine-volume set combines appropriate reading level and fascinating subject matter with quality biographies, statistics, essays, chronologies, document and speech excerpts, and more.

The **African American Reference Library** consists of three separate components:

African American Chronology (two volumes) explores significant social, political, economic, cultural, and educational milestones in black history. Arranged by year and then by month and day, this work spans from 1492, when sailor Pedro Alonzo Niño arrived in the new world with explorer Christopher Columbus, until June 30, 1993, when Los Angeles, California, mayor Tom Bradley stepped down from office after twenty years of service. The *Chronology* features 106 illustrations and maps, extensive cross references directing the reader to related entries, and a cumulative subject index providing easy access to the events and people discussed throughout the volumes.

African American Biography (four Volumes) profiles three hundred African Americans, both living and deceased, prominent in their fields, from civil rights to athletics, politics to literature, entertainment to science, religion to the military. A black-and-white portrait accompanies each entry, and a cumulative subject index lists all individuals by field of endeavor.

African American Almanac (three volumes) provides a comprehensive range of historical and current information on African American life and culture. Organized by subject, the volumes contain 270 black-and-white illustrations, a selected bibliography, and a cumulative subject index.

Comments and suggestions
We welcome your comments on *African American Chronology* as well as your suggestions for topics to be featured in future **African American Reference Library** series. Please write:

Editors, **African American Reference Library**, U·X·L, 835 Penobscot Bldg., Detroit, Michigan 48226-4094; or call toll-free: 1-800-877-4253.

CONTENTS

INTRODUCTION

Out of Africa (300-1619)

The ancestors of most black Americans came from the area of the African continent known as the Western Sudan. This area stretched from the Atlantic Ocean in the west to Lake Chad in the east, and from the Sahara Desert in the north to the Gulf of Guinea in the south.

From about 300 A.D. to the late 1500s, three different empires ruled the Western Sudan. The first was Ghana, followed by Mali and later Songhai. All three grew rich and powerful through trade with their Arab neighbors to the north. The Arabs in turn brought the teachings of Muhammad to the Western Sudan during the seventh and eighth centuries, and Islam soon became an important cultural force.

Under the leadership of Askia Muhammad Touré, whose rule began in 1492, the Western Sudan became the largest and richest country in Africa. Askia Muhammad established an efficient system of centralized government and hired Arab scholars to teach in his empire's two major universities. One of them was located in the city of Timbuktu. It was known throughout the Muslim world as a major center of learning and trade.

In 1528, Askia Muhammad's sons forced their elderly father to give up his throne. For more than fifty years, the brothers fought over who would be in charge as the empire grew weaker and weaker. Finally, in 1590 an invading army from Morocco crushed what was left of the last great black kingdom of West Africa.

The people of West Africa passed along to their descendants a rich tradition of economic success, self-government, religious worship, and cultural expression through music, dance, art, and storytelling. But they also left behind a legacy of slavery. In ancient times, West Africans sold their slaves (many of whom were prisoners of war) to Arab traders. By the early 1500s, however, the West Africans were selling or trading other Africans to Europeans for cloth, rum, and weapons. Portuguese and Spanish colonists then used these slaves on their sugar plantations in Brazil and the West Indies. After 1600, England, France, and the Netherlands also began using slaves in their colonies in North America. Blacks were enslaved in other ways, too. Some were captured by traders in Africa or kidnapped from ships.

Slave voyages across the Atlantic Ocean usually took several months. Since selling more slaves meant making more money, traders and ship captains tried to deliver as many slaves as possible. Conditions on board the boats were horribly crowded and dirty. Except for brief exercise periods, slaves were generally chained together below deck all day and night. Sickness and death were very common. In fact, historians believe that about 12 percent of all slaves died during the Atlantic crossings.

The slave trade between Europe and the Americas lasted until the 1800s. Although the exact number of Africans who were sold into slavery is unknown, the most reliable estimates range from 10,000,000 to 20,000,000. Between 400,000 and 1,200,000 of these people were brought to North America. It was there that they began the long cultural process of becoming African Americans.

Indentured Servants and Slaves (1619-1860)

Blacks were part of the early expeditions to the New World, perhaps even the first voyage of Christopher Columbus. But the first permanent settlers in what would one day be the United States were the twenty blacks dropped off at Jamestown, Virginia, in 1619. Captured in Africa and sold to the highest bidders, they were indentured servants rather than slaves. (Many lower-class whites were kidnapped and forced to suffer the same fate.) As indentured servants, they had to work for someone for a specific period of time, usually seven years. After their term of service ended, some of these free blacks became property owners and community leaders.

African Americans probably lived as indentured servants in the American colonies as late as the mid-1600s. Their total number was very small, however—only about 300 servants, slaves, and free blacks by 1650. But by the time of the American Revolution in 1776, there were about half a million black slaves in the colonies. Almost half of the population in several southern states, including Virginia and Maryland, was black. In South Carolina, blacks outnumbered whites. About 16,000 slaves lived in the North, where Connecticut was the leading New England slave colony. Unlike indentured servants, slaves belonged to their owners, just like farm animals or household goods.

In the South, most slaves helped plant and harvest crops. The typical slave worked on a small farm with one or two other blacks alongside the master and his family. Other slaves worked in and around the master's house instead of out in the fields. In towns and cities, blacks served as messengers, house servants, and craftsmen.

In the North, farming was not as important to the economy as it was in the South. Black slaves therefore worked in a wider variety of jobs. They provided skilled and unskilled labor in homes, ships, factories, and shipyards.

Since England had no laws that defined the status of a slave, the colonies made up their own. These "slave codes" protected the property rights of the master. They also made sure white society was guarded against what was considered a strange and savage race of people. Slaves had almost no rights of their own.

Enforcement of the slave codes varied from one area to another, and even from one plantation to another. Slaves who lived in cities and towns were less restricted than slaves who lived in the country, and slaves on small farms enjoyed more freedom than those on huge plantations. It was on some of the larger plantations that blacks who disobeyed or who tried to run away faced cruel punishments.

Despite the risks, some blacks constantly tried to undermine the slavery system. A few chose rather minor ways, including destroying property and faking illness to avoid having to work. Others took bolder steps to overthrow their masters by joining slave revolts. Still others managed to escape. But many—perhaps most—slaves chose not to resist in the face of almost certain failure and even death.

A few slaves won their freedom, especially in the years just after the Revolutionary War. In appreciation for the service of about 5,000 blacks in the colonists' struggle against the British, and in the spirit of liberty and equality inspired by the Declaration of Independence, many masters (especially in the North) freed their slaves. Soon individual states in the North began making slavery illegal. Statesmen such as George Washington and Thomas Jefferson predicted that slavery would eventually disappear from the land as more and more blacks were freed by law or by their masters.

In the rural South, these free blacks did farm work for others or became independent farmers. In urban areas of the North and South, they were factory workers, businessmen, preachers, craftsmen, and personal servants. Many became successful and prosperous. It was not long, however, before some whites grew frightened by the rapid increase in the population of free blacks. Beginning around 1790, several states passed laws restricting free blacks that left them little better off than slaves.

In 1793, a machine patented by Eli Whitney of Massachusetts changed the course of American history, especially for blacks. His invention, called the cotton gin, separated the cotton from the seeds, hull, and other material. Suddenly, raising cotton became much more profitable for southern farmers. As a result, the number of slaves grew from about half a million in 1776 to four million in 1860, just before the outbreak of the American Civil War.

War, Freedom, and Reconstruction (1861-1876)

The Civil War began on April 12, 1861, following an attack by southern troops on Fort Sumter, South Carolina. In the months just before the first cannons were fired, seven states had seceded, or broken away, from the Union. Led by South Carolina, with Mississippi, Florida, Alabama, Georgia, Louisiana, and Texas following soon after, they formed the Confederate States of America.

The disagreements between the North and the South dated back many years. They grew out of a variety of economic and political rivalries and issues, including whether a state had the right to secede from the Union. Slavery was also a source of conflict, but the Civil War was not a war against slavery. President Abraham Lincoln had made it clear that he had no intention of interfering with slavery where it already existed, and he did not approve of blacks fighting in the Union Army. He was, however, determined to keep the Union together.

The first year of the Civil War went badly for the North. The abolitionists (a group of militant reformers who were demanding freedom for black slaves) refused to support a war whose goals did not include ending slavery and allowing black soldiers to serve in combat. By the summer of 1862, President Lincoln realized he had to change his policies or risk defeat. So, on September 22, 1862, he took a major step that he hoped would give a much-needed boost to the Union effort: he issued the Emancipation Proclamation. Effective on January 1, 1863, it declared slaves free in all states and territories then at war with the United States and opened the door for blacks to serve in the Union Army.

About 200,000 blacks ended up fighting for the Union during the Civil War. Although they faced discrimination at every turn, many served with honor (a few became officers) and were even singled out for praise from the president himself. Around 40,000 black troops lost their lives, mostly from disease.

The war finally came to an end on April 9, 1865, when Confederate General Robert E. Lee surrendered to Union General Ulysses S. Grant near the Appomattox Courthouse in Virginia. President Lincoln and most other white northerners were eager to put the country back together again as soon as possible. His plans to reorganize and rebuild the defeated South, a program known as Reconstruction, were especially generous and lenient. But less than a week after the war ended, Lincoln was assassinated. His successor, Andrew Johnson, was a southerner who promised to continue Lincoln's policies in the spirit of reconciliation. But even though President Johnson supported outlawing slavery, he made little effort to grant blacks civil rights protection or give them the vote. He tolerated anti-black violence in some southern states, and he did nothing to stop white governments in the South from passing laws similar to the old slave codes.

Republican leaders in Congress were afraid that President Johnson was just making it easier for white Democrats to gain control once again throughout the South. So they came up with a much harsher Reconstruction program. Under their plan, the southern states would not be allowed to rejoin the Union until the Republicans had become stronger and until blacks were given the vote and guaranteed civil rights.

In 1866 and 1867, the Republicans took over the Reconstruction effort from President Johnson and began pushing their radical reforms through the House of Representatives and the Senate. In 1870, for example, the Fifteenth Amendment to the Constitution was ratified, or approved, and blacks were finally granted the right to vote. For the first time, they participated in large numbers in southern politics, electing members of their own race and sympathetic whites to offices ranging from city councilman to U.S. senator.

The Spirit of Reconstruction Fades (1877-1900)

By the mid-1870s, the Republicans had begun to lose interest in radical Reconstruction efforts. Their presence in the South came to an end for the most part following the presidential election of 1876. In this controversial contest, southern Democrats agreed to certify Republican candidate Rutherford Hayes as president if the Republicans promised two things. First of all, they had to give more federal aid to the South. Secondly, they had to withdraw the federal troops who were still stationed in the South to enforce Reconstruction policies. The Republicans accepted the Democrats' conditions, and Hayes became president.

The next two decades were among the darkest years in African American history. Abandoned by the Republican party and stripped of the protection of federal troops, blacks now had to deal on their own with southern whites who acted quickly to take control again. One state after another legalized segregation and discrimination, even passing laws making it almost impossible for blacks to vote. In a series of decisions during the 1880s and 1890s, the U.S. Supreme Court upheld these new laws and struck down older ones that had guaranteed blacks certain civil rights.

Meanwhile, the national government followed a "hands-off" policy toward the South. It was not long before blacks were living under conditions very similar to those they had known under slavery. Making matters even worse was a rise in violence against blacks, especially lynching. But out of this grim atmosphere came two new leaders who would have a major impact on African American history—Booker T. Washington and W.E.B. Du Bois.

The Age of Booker T. Washington (1901-1917)

As the founder and head of Alabama's Tuskegee Institute, Booker T. Washington was already famous when he spoke at the 1895 Cotton States International Exposition in Atlanta, Georgia. In his speech, which came to be known as the "Atlanta Compromise," he advised blacks to stop demanding political power and social equality. Instead, he asked whites to help blacks advance economically through education, primarily in the areas of agriculture and industrial arts. Once blacks showed how much they could contribute to the American economy, Washington reasoned, whites would grant equality to blacks out of respect and gratitude.

This formula for racial peace and progress received widespread approval among whites in the North as well as the South. Many blacks also supported it. But others strongly disagreed with Washington and his "accommodationist" ideas, which expected blacks to accept things the way they were and wait patiently for change.

One of Washington's harshest critics was scholar W.E.B. Du Bois. In mid-1905, a group of black "radicals" led by Du Bois and publisher William Monroe Trotter met at Niagara Falls, Canada. There they called for immediate and aggressive action to end racial discrimination in the United States. The group held other meetings throughout America and added members from nearly every major city.

In 1909, following anti-black riots in Texas, Georgia, and Illinois, the so-called "Niagara Movement" merged with a group of white liberals to form the National Association for the Advancement of Colored People (NAACP). Its goal was to obtain racial equality for all Americans. Soon it had earned a reputation as the most militant civil rights organization in the United States.

Despite the efforts of the Niagara Movement and the NAACP, Booker T. Washington remained very popular among most blacks, wealthy whites, and national and local political figures. But after his death in 1915, there was no one person powerful enough or respected enough to take his place as the spokesman for black America. So several different people, including some members of the NAACP, shared the leadership role.

Between War and Depression (1918-1932)

For the most part, white Americans opposed the demands of these new black leaders. Racial oppression continued, including police brutality, lynchings, and legal discrimination in employment, housing, education, and voting. Even black soldiers who served during World War I experienced harassment at home and overseas. After the war, during the summer of 1919, the United States was rocked by some of the worst race riots in the country's history.

The 1920s were a time of disappointment and despair for black Americans. Yet it was also a decade of great creativity and energy. In New York City's Harlem, for example, a group of black writers and artists began producing works that showed the realities of ghetto life and cried out for relief from oppression. (The movement came to be known as the "Harlem Renaissance.") Across the rest of the country, black singers, musicians, and composers entertained audiences with their talents.

Meanwhile, West Indian immigrant Marcus Garvey appealed to quite a few dissatisfied blacks with a revival of black nationalism. He stressed race pride and urged his followers to return to Africa. Garvey's dream of establishing a new empire faded when he went to prison for mail fraud.

The Great Depression that hit the United States in 1929 was especially hard on blacks, most of whom were already struggling to make a living. Discrimination made their suffering even worse. When Franklin Roosevelt took office as president in 1933, American blacks were more than ready for the "New Deal" he had promised to those who voted for him.

A New Deal—A New Life? (1933-1940)

President Roosevelt's various recovery and reform programs—such as the Civilian Conservation Corps (CCC), the National Youth Administration (NYA), and the Works Progress Administration (WPA)—helped blacks as well as whites. But because many of them were supervised by whites at the state and local level, blacks could not help but wonder if they were receiving their fair share of benefits, especially in the South. Nevertheless, they welcomed the New Deal as a sign of hope and progress.

There were other reasons for optimism, too. Although President Roosevelt relied primarily on white advisors, he also turned to a group that came to be known as his "Black Cabinet." Among its members were prominent blacks in a variety of fields, including educator Mary McLeod Bethune and political scientist Ralph Bunche. They kept the president informed about issues of interest to African Americans.

War Again (1941-1945)

In 1939, the outbreak of World War II in Europe sent many southern blacks north in search of good-paying factory jobs. But discrimination shut them out of many companies. Finally, after blacks threatened to march in protest on Washington, D.C., President Roosevelt issued an order forbidding discrimination in defense-related industries.

Once the United States entered the war in 1941, hundreds of thousands of black Americans served in the armed forces. Their distinguished role in the victory, along with the growing black population in American cities, a rise in the literacy rate among blacks, and increasing economic opportunities, inspired new efforts to end racial discrimination. Leading the way was the NAACP.

The Attack against Segregation (1945-1953)

Basing their arguments on rights guaranteed in the Constitution, NAACP lawyers began challenging segregation and discrimination in the courts. They took many of their cases all the way to the U.S. Supreme Court, winning several important decisions before the war. But the big push came after the war, when the NAACP slowly but surely demolished legalized segregation and discrimination in all areas of American life—voting, housing, transportation, education, and recreation, to name just a few. The Supreme Court's decisions on school segregation, including the landmark *Brown v. Board of Education* in 1954, were especially important. They brought about changes that launched a whole new era in African American history, the era of civil rights.

"The Second Reconstruction" (1954-1964)

As the courts destroyed what remained of legalized segregation, other branches of government took action, too. Congress passed laws to make sure white southerners could not cheat blacks out of their right to vote. President Harry S. Truman banned segregation in the armed forces. Later, President Dwight Eisenhower ended discrimination in federal housing assistance programs. In addition, civil rights committees assembled to investigate and report on injustices.

Even though segregation and discrimination were against the law, they had not just disappeared. So blacks turned their attention to fighting the kind of bias that was common in restaurants and hotels, on buses, and in other public places. Boycotts and sit-ins became popular and effective ways to protest. In fact, blacks achieved so much in the area of civil rights from 1954 until 1964 that some people started to think of the decade as "The Second Reconstruction." To them, the work of the first Reconstruction after the Civil War had been left unfinished, and now was the time for it to continue.

"The Second Reconstruction" Fades (1964-1973)

The landmark Civil Rights Law of 1964 had barely gone into effect when a serious race riot erupted in Harlem. Racial disturbances occurred that summer in several other northern ghettos. A year later, during the summer of 1965, the black ghetto of Watts in Los Angeles, California, exploded in violence. For the next two summers, dozens of other riots broke out across the country. Many were sparked by fights between blacks and white police officers.

A special presidential commission looked into the reasons behind the riots. Its members found that despite all of the court decisions, sit-ins, marches, and boycotts, the average black American was still living with the crippling effects of segregation, discrimination, and, above all, racism. The 1968 assassination of civil rights leader Martin Luther King, Jr.—a champion of nonviolence—added to the sense of despair most blacks felt.

Some continued their search for dignity and justice as part of the Black Consciousness Movement. With its themes of "Black Is Beautiful" and "I'm Black and I'm Proud," the Black Consciousness Movement inspired new calls for black nationalism and black separatism.

"The Second Reconstruction" Betrayed (1973-1992)

For the most part, the 1970s and 1980s cast a shadow over the dreams of black Americans for racial justice and equality. With the exception of Jimmy Carter's presidency from 1976 to 1980, it was a time when blacks first felt neglected, then threatened. There was little attempt to enforce existing civil rights laws, for example, and very few blacks were named to top positions in the federal government. (They did make progress in local politics, however, especially in the South.) Schools and businesses felt less pressure to recruit minorities to make up for the unfair practices of the past, especially after white men began to complain about "reverse discrimination." And Republican presidents from Richard Nixon through George Bush suggested that blacks' problems stemmed less from racism than from a need for more initiative, self-reliance, and economic development within the black community.

Jimmy Carter's election to the presidency in 1976 held out the promise of a new way of thinking. While he did name several blacks to high-level positions, President Carter came under fire for not doing enough to help the vast majority of African Americans. A shaky economy marked by high inflation and gasoline shortages hit blacks especially hard during his administration. The Iran hostage crisis of 1979 added to the nation's depressed mood and paved the way for a return to Republican control of the White House in 1980.

Under the new president, Ronald Reagan, blacks once again found themselves shut out of the highest levels of government. Although he insisted that his moves to strengthen the economy helped all Americans, black as well as white, President Reagan opposed or ignored many issues of interest to black Americans. He appointed conservative judges to various federal courts (including the Supreme Court) who struck down many programs that had been designed to make up for past discrimination against minorities.

At first, black Americans who felt abandoned by their government turned instead to the major civil rights organizations for leadership. But the marches and court decisions that had been so effective during the 1950s and 1960s did not have the same impact during the 1970s and 1980s, and the riots had not led to any major improvements. Many blacks seemed resigned to the fact that America was still a nation of two societies—one black, one white—separate and unequal. The increase in racially motivated violence against blacks during the 1980s supported this belief that racism was alive and well in America.

Discouraged by these setbacks, some blacks decided that the only way to make progress on issues of importance to African Americans was to reject traditional politics. A few looked into alternative movements, including the Nation of Islam and Afrocentrism, which stressed the value of black culture and the black experience (especially its African roots).

One who chose a different path was Jesse Jackson, a minister and veteran civil rights activist who had become the most popular national black leader since Martin Luther King, Jr. In 1984, he campaigned for the Democratic nomination for president of the United States. Even though he lost in a bitter fight to former vice-president Walter Mondale (who later lost the presidential election to Ronald Reagan), Jackson inspired thousands of blacks at a time when they had just about given up on politics. And his candidacy proved that it was possible for an African American to seek the nomination of a major party.

By the late 1980s, blacks were mayors of almost all of the country's larger cities and some of its smaller ones, too. Black representation in state legislatures, school boards, and state courts was also increasing, especially in the South. Encouraged by these trends, Jesse Jackson decided to run again for the Democratic presidential nomination in 1988.

This time, Jackson made a special effort to reach out to the people who had not supported him in 1984. He was much more successful in the primaries and ended up finishing a strong second in the delegate count. This gave him enough power to help shape the Democratic platform, or its statement of policies and principles. He was also able to make sure that blacks received some high-ranking jobs in the party. Most of all, his success continued to reduce the feeling among many African Americans that they had been shut out of politics at the national level. But at election time, the Republicans once again captured the White House.

After George Bush took office as president in January, 1989, some blacks thought he would reverse the trends of the Reagan years and revive the "Second Reconstruction." The early signs were hopeful. He named General Colin Powell head of the Joint Chiefs of Staff and made Dr. Louis Sullivan secretary of Health and Human Services. He repeatedly expressed his admiration for the ideals of Martin Luther King, Jr., and observed the national holiday honoring the slain civil rights activist. And in 1990, he welcomed African National Congress leader Nelson Mandela to the White House.

But by mid-1990, many blacks had begun to question President Bush's sincerity on issues of importance to African Americans. For example, they thought he was too eager to support the white minority government in South Africa. They were outraged when he vetoed the 1991 Civil Rights Bill because it contained what he felt were unconstitutional employment quotas. In addition, many blacks did not support America's involvement in the Persian Gulf War or the nomination of Clarence Thomas to the U.S. Supreme Court.

Years of anger and frustration came to a head in April, 1992, after four white Los Angeles policemen were found not guilty in the 1991 beating of black motorist Rodney King. Los Angeles experienced the worst riot in American history. Disturbances broke out in several other cities, too. Not since the civil rights era of the 1950s and 1960s had there been so much protest. And for a short time at least, the dismal conditions faced by urban blacks received national attention.

Toward a Black Agenda (1993 and Beyond)

By the time of the 1992 presidential election, the ongoing economic recession, not the Los Angeles riot, was the topic on everyone's mind. That November, a large number of white voters joined with an overwhelming majority of black voters to demand change. They turned Republican George Bush out of office after only one term and elected Democrat Bill Clinton instead. Also as a result of the elections, the Congressional Black Caucus grew from twenty-five members to thirty-nine. For the first time, the group appeared to be in a position to exercise a considerable amount of power, especially with a Democrat in the White House.

Although President Clinton chose several blacks and other minorities for positions in his cabinet, many African Americans adopted a "wait-and-see" attitude toward the new administration. Some questioned the sincerity of Clinton's commitment to a "Black Agenda." They pointed out that he campaigned heavily among middle-class whites, avoided Jesse Jackson and other more outspoken black leaders, and never presented any concrete plans for dealing with problems unique to the black community.

In fact, President Clinton stumbled badly on a number of issues of importance to African Americans. Many blacks were upset by his decision to return Haitian refugees to their country—a policy he had condemned during the campaign. Others were disappointed by the defeat of his job creation bill, which they blamed on an ineffective White House strategy. Battles over the proposed budget for social programs also alienated many black leaders as the president ignored African

American politicians and instead looked for support among moderate and conservative white Democrats.

Perhaps the biggest blow, however, came when President Clinton withdrew Lani Guinier's nomination to head the civil rights division of the Justice Department. Within days, angry members of the Congressional Black Caucus responded by announcing that the group was planning to "reassess" its relationship with the White House. As everyone continues to watch the direction President Clinton takes, black Americans in particular can be counted on to take up their concerns with both Congress and the new administration.

—Alton Hornsby, Jr. and Deborah Gillan Straub, August 1993

PHOTO CREDITS

The photographs and illustrations appearing in *African American Chronology* were received from the following sources:

On the covers: **AP/Wide World Photos.**

Archive Photos: page 35; **Schomberg Center for Research in Black Culture, The New York Public Library, Astor, Lenox and Tilden Foundations:** pages 49, 50, 216; **National Archives:** pages 51, 99; **The Granger Collection, New York:** page 54; **AP/Wide World Photos:** pages 62, 70, 74, 82, 93, 106, 107, 110, 112, 117, 119, 125, 128, 135, 136, 138, 141, 189, 190, 219, 220, 236, 252, 258, 261, 266, 271, 304, 306, 313, 316, 319, 321, 330, 333, 356; **The Bettmann Archive:** pages 63, 72; **UPI/Bettmann Newsphotos:** pages 68, 95, 114, 131, 133, 140, 142, 146, 147, 171, 205; **Bethune Museum and Archive:** page 77; **Photograph by Merrill A. Roberts, Jr:** page 81; **Photograph by Cecil Layne:** page 85; **Hurok Attractions:** page 86; **U.S. Air Force:** page 88; **U.S. Navy:** page 90; **New York Times Pictures:** page 103; **Bill Sparrow/*Encore* Magazine:** page 105; **Photograph by Carl Nesfeld:** page 126; **United Nations:** page 129; **Ace Creative Photos:** page 134; *Downbeat* magazine: page 143; **Photograph by Chester Higgins, Jr:** page 166; *New York Amsterdam News:* page 197; **Keystone Photos:** page 203; **William Morris Agency:** page 305; **(c) Scott Cunningham 1987:** page 307.

AFRICAN AMERICAN
CHRONOLOGY

1973   **May 29.** Tom Bradley was elected the new mayor of the city of Los Angeles, California. A veteran city councilman, he defeated Mayor Sam Yorty, who was seeking a fourth four-year term. Bradley had lost to Yorty in the 1969 mayoral race. (Also see entry dated June 30, 1993.)

July 2. The National Black Network (NBN), the nation's first radio news network owned and operated by blacks, began operations with hourly newscasts to forty affiliated stations. Although based in New York City, the NBN planned to provide news stories of interest to blacks everywhere.

August 15. The National Black Feminist Organization (NBFO) was founded in New York City. Several other cities were also home to their own chapters, including Chicago, Illinois; Cleveland, Ohio; and San Francisco, California. Among its founders was Eleanor Holmes Norton, a member of the New York City Human Rights Commission.

October 16. Maynard Jackson was elected the first black mayor of Atlanta, Georgia. The thirty-five-year-old attorney and vice mayor of the city defeated white mayor Sam Massell in a campaign that saw Massell bring up the race issue to attract white voters. Although Jackson had angered many whites with his outspoken criticism of alleged police brutality in Atlanta, he ended up appealing to voters of both races at election time.

Jackson's election signaled a shift of political power from white to black in Atlanta as African Americans achieved equality on the eighteen-member city council and a slight majority on the nine-member school board.

October. As the 1973 professional baseball season came to an end, star centerfielder Willie Mays closed out his long career in the majors. He had won national acclaim for his fielding heroics and for his powerful bat during nearly twenty years of play in the National League, first with the Giants (in New York and San Francisco) and finally with the New York Mets. On September 25, New York City honored Mays in special ceremonies at Shea Stadium as 55,000 fans cheered the black star.

That same fall, Reggie Jackson of the Oakland Athletics was unanimously selected as the Most Valuable Player (MVP) in the World Series, which saw Oakland defeat

187

the New York Mets. Only three other black players had won the MVP award in previous years—Bob Gibson of the St. Louis Cardinals in 1964 and 1967, Frank Robinson of the Baltimore Orioles in 1966, and Roberto Clemente of the Pittsburgh Pirates in 1971.

November 6. Michigan state senator Coleman Young defeated a white former police commissioner to become the first black mayor of Detroit, Michigan.

By the end of the year, blacks headed almost 100 of the nation's 18,000 local governments, including such major cities as Los Angeles, California; Washington D.C.; Newark, New Jersey; Cincinnati, Ohio; and Atlanta, Georgia.

1974　**February 15.** The *San Francisco Chronicle* reported that two black escaped convicts had been identified as leaders of the Symbionese Liberation Army (SLA). The SLA was an interracial group of radical revolutionaries that had made news for allegedly kidnapping white newspaper heiress Patricia Hearst.

One of the SLA leaders was Donald D. DeFreeze, who called himself Field Marshal Cinque on tapes he sent to the Hearst family. He had escaped from California's Soledad State Prison on March 5, 1973. The other black SLA leader was identified as Thero M. Wheeler, who had escaped from Vacaville State Prison in August, 1973.

The newspaper report traced the two men's involvement with the SLA to their memberships in the Black Cultural Association (BCA) at Vacaville State Prison. The BCA was an inmate group that sponsored cultural activities, educational programs, and pre-release preparation projects. White SLA members Russell Little, Jo Ann Little, and William Wolfe had reportedly gained control of the BCA while working as tutors at the prison.

April 8. Atlanta Braves baseball star Henry (Hank) Aaron hit his 715th career home run at Atlanta Stadium, breaking Babe Ruth's old record to become the all-time leading home run slugger.

May 16. Four young black men were charged with the random "Zebra" killings of twelve whites that had left the city of San Francisco, California, tense for five months.

All but one were arrested during a massive police manhunt on May 1 known as "Operation Zebra." During "Operation Zebra," San Francisco police had stopped and searched about 600 black men who matched the description of the killer as young and slim. A federal judge later ruled the searches unconstitutional and ordered authorities to stop questioning black men just because they fit the police profile.

Hank Aaron celebrates after hitting his 715th career home run

May 16. The U.S. Senate approved a bill to limit court-ordered busing to achieve school desegregation.

The major new feature of the bill stated that students should not be bused beyond the next nearest school to their homes. It also required officials to consider other alternatives to achieve desegregation before they turned to busing. The bill, however, pointed out that these new limitations were not intended to stop judges from ordering busing if it became necessary to enforce the equal rights provisions of the U.S. Constitution.

May 24. Edward Kennedy "Duke" Ellington, one of America's greatest musicians and composers, died in New York at the age of seventy-four.

Ellington was born in 1899 in Washington, D.C., and grew up there. Gifted from childhood with a talent for music, he began playing the piano at age seven. He especially liked to experiment with unusual chords and sounds, which finally led his frustrated teacher to give up on him.

But Ellington kept playing on his own and learned to imitate and memorize pieces he heard other people play. He composed his first song at seventeen and began

Duke Ellington

playing professionally at eighteen. By then, he was already known as "Duke" thanks to a friend who thought it suited his stylish clothes, sophisticated manners, and elegant way of talking.

In 1922, after establishing a reputation as an outstanding jazz pianist around the Washington area, Ellington headed north to New York City with a few of his bandmates. There they played in Harlem's best-known nightspot, the Cotton Club, where their performances were carried live on radio and broadcast from coast to coast. By the end of the decade, they were famous all over the country.

During the 1930s and early 1940s, Ellington and his orchestra were the most popular black jazz band in the United States. After the 1940s, when jazz declined in popularity, his orchestra was one of the few that survived. In fact, in the mid- to late 1950s, a new generation of fans "discovered" Ellington, and for the rest of his life he remained at or near the top of the jazz world.

Besides being a popular and respected musician, Ellington was a noted composer. He wrote most of the material his orchestra recorded, for example, and he also sold other pieces to music publishers. Over the course of his entire career, Ellington wrote or cowrote more than 2,000 compositions, including "Mood Indigo," "Take the 'A' Train," "Don't Get around Much Anymore," "Satin Doll," and "Caravan." In later years he composed several orchestral pieces, tone poems, jazz masses, operas, and scores for film, television, and ballets.

Among Ellington's numerous awards were the NAACP's Spingarn Medal, the French Legion of Merit (France's highest honor), and America's highest civilian honor, the Medal of Freedom, which he received in 1970.

Reacting to news of his death, a spokesperson for the NAACP noted: "Few composers have attained the greatness of stature that was the Duke's at the time of his death. Prolific, versatile, and popular, the Duke claimed the hearts of a wide range of followers, black and white, rich and poor. He was indomitable." Although he was sometimes criticized for not taking on an active role in the civil rights movement, Ellington himself claimed that "protest and pride in the Negro have been the most significant themes in what we've done." In fact, his composition "My People" was a musical salute to African Americans.

May 27. About 1,000 demonstrators marched through downtown Atlanta, Georgia, demanding that the city's controversial police chief, John Inman, be fired. The marchers were led by veteran protester Hosea Williams, formerly a top assistant to Martin Luther King, Jr.

Many Atlanta blacks considered Inman to be a racist, and they had wanted to force him from his job for a long time. Atlanta's black mayor, Maynard Jackson, had tried to fire Inman on May 3, but a county judge stopped him from doing so. (Also see entry dated June 26, 1974.)

June 16. Lawrence W. Bottoms, a minister from Decatur, Georgia, was elected as the first black moderator of the General Assembly of the Presbyterian Church of the United States.

A sixty-six-year-old native of Selma, Alabama, Bottoms had long experience as a pastor and leader of Georgia's black Presbyterians. He was also a strong supporter of racial integration and tolerance. In his new job, he headed the branch of the Presbyterian Church that had split away from the main church to defend slavery before the Civil War.

June 21. The U.S. Department of Health, Education, and Welfare (HEW) accepted university desegregation plans from eight states—Arkansas, Florida, Georgia, Maryland, North Carolina, Oklahoma, Pennsylvania, and Virginia. HEW officials rejected Mississippi's plan, and Louisiana had refused to submit one in protest against the federal government's attempts to force the state to merge its black and white universities.

At the time, black educators and civil rights leaders across the country were becoming more and more divided over the question of desegregation at the college level. Many black educators and students feared losses of jobs, social status, and some of their cultural heritage if historically black universities merged with white universities in the name of desegregation. On the other hand, many civil rights leaders continued to call for complete desegregation, no matter what the consequences.

June 21. A U.S. District Court judge in Memphis, Tennessee, began a preliminary hearing to determine whether or not James Earl Ray, the confessed assassin of Dr. Martin Luther King, Jr., should receive a new trial.

In 1969, Ray had been sentenced to a prison term of ninety-nine years for the slaying of King on April 4, 1968. He had asked for a new trial on the grounds that he was pressured into pleading guilty by his original attorneys because they had financial ties to a man who was writing one of the first books to be published about King's death. Also, Ray's new attorney claimed that his client was innocent of King's murder and that two professional assassins hired by four "wealthy, socially prominent Americans" had killed the noted civil rights leader. (Also see entries dated April 4, 1968; March 10, 1969; January 8, 1970; June 29, 1974; October 29, 1974; and February 28, 1975.)

June 22. The U.S. Navy reported that an investigation showed no basis for accusations of racial discrimination made by a group of black sailors a week before.

Fifty-five sailors had refused to return to the aircraft carrier U.S.S. *Midway* when it left the Yokosuka Naval Base near Tokyo, Japan. Eight of them asked the U.S. Congress to investigate conditions aboard the ship and demanded that the ship's captain be replaced. They complained of being forced to perform dangerous work, long duty hours, and torture in the brig. Navy officials reasoned that since there was no evidence of racial bias, the men were "being misled by private organizations" trying to exploit them for "their own purpose."

The *Midway* incident was the latest in a series of racially related events involving black armed forces personnel.

June 26. In Atlanta, Georgia, police officers armed with clubs broke up a march of about 250 blacks and arrested fourteen people. Among those arrested was the leader of the demonstration, Hosea Williams, president of the local chapter of the

Southern Christian Leadership Conference (SCLC). Seven people, including three police officers, were injured in the disturbance. It was the first violent conflict in Atlanta since the riots of the 1960s.

Marchers had been protesting the killing by police of a seventeen-year-old black youth the previous weekend. They were also continuing to demand the removal of the city's white police chief, John Inman, whom they felt was racist. The blacks arrested were charged with parading without permits.

Inman defended the force used against the marchers, but the city's black mayor, Maynard Jackson, described it as excessive. The latest incident occurred as the Georgia Supreme Court was considering whether the city of Atlanta could legally fire Inman. Many of the city's whites saw him as a staunch defender of "law and order," but many blacks considered him a racist. (See also entry dated May 27, 1974.)

June 29. Robert Livingston, the attorney handling the legal appeals of James Earl Ray, the convicted assassin of Martin Luther King, Jr., told newsmen he was convinced that a conspiracy existed in the slaying of the civil rights leader.

Livingston claimed that on March 22, 1974, he was contacted by someone who said that he and two other men were prepared to testify that four prominent black and white men had hired them to kill King. Earlier, law enforcement officials had ruled out a conspiracy theory in the assassination of the famed civil rights leader. They continued to insist that James Earl Ray had acted alone. (Also see entries dated April 4, 1968; March 10, 1969; January 8, 1970; June 21, 1974; October 29, 1974; and February 28, 1975.)

June 30. In Atlanta, Georgia, a young black man interrupted worship services at Ebenezer Baptist Church with gunfire, killing Mrs. Martin Luther King, Sr. (the mother of the slain civil rights leader), and a church deacon and wounding another worshipper.

Other church members (including Mrs. King's grandson, Derek King) immediately grabbed the gunman, who was identified as Marcus Chenault of Dayton, Ohio. Chenault told police that he had orders from "his god" to go to Atlanta and kill Martin Luther King, Sr., the father of the civil rights leader. Instead, he fired at Mrs. King and the others as she played the organ.

Officials described Chenault as an Ohio State University dropout who had become deeply involved in a small religious cult that claimed blacks were descendants of the original Jews. The cult reportedly believed that black Christian ministers had misled African Americans and that they were to blame for many of the social and economic problems of blacks.

On July 3, more than 600 mourners, including First Lady Betty Ford, Mrs. Nelson Rockefeller, Georgia governor Jimmy Carter, and Atlanta mayor Maynard Jackson, attended the funeral services for Mrs. King in Atlanta. (Also see entry dated September 12, 1974.)

July 4. Four to five thousand protesters, led by black Communist Angela Davis and SCLC president Ralph David Abernathy, marched on the North Carolina state capitol in Raleigh to call for an end to the death penalty in that state. The march was organized by the National Alliance Against Racist and Political Repression. Members of the group called it "a rebirth of the civil rights movement of the 1960s, but on a higher level."

During the march, twelve picketers representing the American Nazi Party, the Ku Klux Klan, and similar groups stood alongside the route holding signs urging segregation forever. They also showed their support for Alabama governor George Wallace for president of the United States. Raleigh police kept the two groups apart. Although there was much jeering and shouting, there were no major incidents or arrests.

July 5. Approximately 200 blacks marched about seven miles along Highway 41 in Talbot County, Georgia, to protest the shooting of a young black man by the white police chief of Woodland.

Willie Gene Carraker, a twenty-five-year-old black resident of Woodland, died from gunshot wounds on June 29, 1974. The black man's family accused Police Chief Doug Watson of aggravated assault and murder in connection with Carraker's slaying. A local justice of the peace later dismissed the charges.

During the march on July 5, black protesters demanded that the chief be prosecuted and removed from office. As a spokesman for the group said, "We are sick and tired of white folks shooting down our young men every weekend. We are sick and tired of being treated like second class citizens."

The Woodland city attorney defended the decision to dismiss charges against Chief

Watson. He also pointed out that the incident could be investigated by a grand jury.

August. Beverly Johnson became the first black model to appear on the cover of *Vogue* magazine.

Johnson had won a full academic scholarship to Boston's Northeastern University but left after her freshman year to become a model. She was soon one of the world's top high fashion models as well as an outspoken, career-minded woman. When a radio host once commented that she was the "biggest black model in the business," she replied, "No, I'm not. I'm the biggest model—period."

September 7. Owners of the National Black Network (NBN), the nation's first radio network owned and operated by blacks for a black audience, announced plans to expand its coverage with a twenty-four-hour-a-day black news service.

September 12. Marcus Chenault was convicted and sentenced to death for the murder of Mrs. Martin Luther King, Sr., mother of the slain civil rights leader. The Fulton County (Georgia) Court jury rejected Chenault's insanity plea in delivering their verdict. The State Supreme Court later upheld his conviction and sentence on appeal.

Students leave Boston's Hyde Park High School after fighting breaks out over forced busing

September 12-October 31. The city of Boston, Massachusetts, began a program of busing to achieve school desegregation. The boycotts and demonstrations it sparked were similar to the ones that had occurred in the South during the early years of fierce opposition to school integration.

When the busing began on September 12, many white and

black parents kept their children at home. Black children attending some of the newly integrated schools, particularly in the white neighborhoods of South Boston, Hyde Park, and Dorchester, faced jeers from angry white parents.

On September 16, a crowd of white teenagers and mothers clashed with police officers at South Boston High School. Twenty-two people were arrested during the confrontation. Racial violence continued in Boston for the next few weeks as fights broke out between students at several different schools. The protests against desegregation included one staged by a member of the American Nazi Party in front of the federal building in Boston.

The traumatic experience of desegregating schools in Boston highlighted the increasing white opposition to massive school desegregation in the North. Many observers also felt it was a sign that Americans were taking several steps backward in the area of race relations.

September 27. In Richmond, Virginia, a U.S. District judge ordered the American Tobacco Company and Local 182 of the Tobacco Workers' International Union to allow blacks and females to "bump" white employees with less seniority.

The judge had found the company and the union guilty of racial and sexual discrimination in violation of the Civil Rights Act of 1964. This is believed to be the first time a court approved "bumping" in a civil rights case.

October 3. The Cleveland Indians named baseball star Frank Robinson the first black manager in the major leagues. At a press conference that day announcing the appointment, Robinson said: "To say that this is a proud day for me would be an understatement.... If I had one wish in the world today, that wish would be to have Jackie Robinson here to see this happen.... I don't think I could have stood the pressure or have gone through what Jackie had to." Jackie Robinson (who was no relation to Frank) had become the major league's first black baseball player in 1947.

The only man in baseball history to be named Most Valuable Player in both the American and National Leagues, Frank Robinson had accumulated nearly 3,000 hits, including 574 home runs, before breaking the 105-year-old managerial color-line. On the first day of the 1975 season, he added his own name to the lineup as a designated hitter and went out and hit his 575th home run.

October 3. At St. Michael's Cemetery in Queens, New York, a bronze plaque honoring ragtime composer Scott Joplin was placed on his grave more than fifty years after his death. Paid for by the American Society of Composers, Authors, and Publishers (ASCAP), the plaque finally acknowledged the contributions of a man who once seemed destined to rest in obscurity.

Frank Robinson

A native of Texas, Joplin was born in 1868. He showed a talent for music even as a child, and by the time he was in his teens, he had already hit the road to play piano in the bars and bordellos of towns along the Mississippi River.

Joplin settled in Missouri in 1894, and there he began studying and composing music. His first hit came in 1899 with "The Maple Leaf Rag." He followed it up with other short ragtime pieces that were also very popular.

Joplin then headed to New York to try his luck at publishing longer and more serious works, including a fully orchestrated folk opera called *Treemonisha*. But no one would consider backing a black pianist who had learned his craft in midwestern saloons. Joplin finally had to publish *Treemonisha* himself and even staged an unsuccessful piano version of it in Harlem.

These professional failures plus health problems left Joplin battered emotionally and physically. In 1916, he was committed to a state mental hospital and died a year later.

By then, people had lost interest in ragtime music. Joplin himself was forgotten by all but a few devoted fans until the early 1970s, when classical music critics raved about a newly released recording of his compositions. Then an African American musical theater group staged a full-scale production of *Treemonisha*. Finally, in 1974, some of Joplin's ragtime pieces were featured in the popular film *The Sting*.

By 1975, a ragtime revival was in full swing, and Joplin's music was at the head of it. Scholars began reconsidering his place in American music history and decided that he deserved to be ranked among the country's most distinguished composers. In 1976, the Pulitzer Prize committee agreed and awarded Joplin a special citation for his contributions to American music.

October 12. Frank L. Stanley, Sr., owner and publisher of the *Louisville Defender* and veteran civil rights activist, died in Louisville, Kentucky. He was sixty-eight.

A native of Chicago, Illinois, Stanley moved to Louisville with his family when he was six years old. He later attended Atlanta University and the University of Cincinnati.

In 1933, Stanley went to work for the *Louisville Defender* as a reporter. Three years later he became editor, general manager, and a part owner of the newspaper. Under his leadership, the *Defender* received more than thirty-five journalism awards, including the President's Special Service Award of the National Newspaper Publishers' Association (NNPA) in 1970 and the coveted Russwurm Award in 1974. Stanley was a co-founder of the NNPA and served five separate terms as its president.

In the area of civil rights, Stanley drafted the legislation that led to the desegregation of state universities in Kentucky in 1950. Ten years later he wrote the bill that created the Kentucky Commission on Human Rights. He also served as one of the original members of the commission.

In 1950, the *Louisville Courier-Journal* noted Stanley's influence on race relations in Kentucky in an editorial marking the 25th anniversary of the *Defender*. "Much of the credit for the even and amiable pace Kentucky has maintained in its working out of race relations problems must be given the *Defender*," observed the editorial writer. Stanley was the force behind the newspaper's role in that achievement.

October 29. During a federal court hearing in Memphis, Tennessee, James Earl Ray insisted that he had not assassinated Dr. Martin Luther King, Jr.

Ray did admit that he had purchased the gun that killed King and that he had rented the room in the building from which the shot was fired. But he said he was not the one who had pulled the trigger. Ray referred to a mysterious figure he called "another party" as the possible killer in a conspiracy to murder the civil rights leader.

Prosecuting attorneys had a hard time finding out any more details from Ray because of a ruling by the presiding judge. He said that the prosecuting attorneys could only ask Ray questions about what he had told his former lawyers. If Ray had failed to discuss a particular subject with them, it was off-limits for the prosecuting attorneys, too.

Ray was seeking his freedom or a new trial on the grounds that his original lawyers misled him into pleading guilty at his 1968 trial. He claimed that they had conspired with a writer named William Bradford Huie for such a plea so that Huie could make money writing a book on King's assassination. (Also see entries dated April 4, 1968; March 10, 1969; January 8, 1970; June 21, 1974; June 29, 1974; and February 28, 1975.)

October 29. Thirty-two-year-old Muhammad Ali regained the heavyweight boxing championship by defeating George Foreman in the African city of Kinshasa, Zaire.

November 2. Police announced they were seeking Huey Newton, co-founder of the Black Panther Party, on charges of murder.

He was accused of shooting seventeen-year-old Kathleen Smith in the head during an argument. The dispute occurred on a street in Oakland, California, on August 6, 1974. Newton had jumped bail and disappeared on August 23. The murder charge was the latest in a long history of encounters between Newton and the law. (Also see entries dated September 8, 1968; May 29, 1970; August, 1970; August 8, 1971; December 15, 1971; and August 22, 1989.)

1975   **January 2-26.** Several reports in the nation's newspapers revealed that the Central Intelligence Agency (CIA) and Federal Bureau of Investigation (FBI) had been spying on black individuals and organizations for many years.

The *New York Times* reported on January 2 that the CIA had been collecting information on singer Eartha Kitt since 1956. The CIA's files contained information on her personal life and habits, including her support of Martin Luther King, Jr., and his civil rights activities. They also claimed that she had once danced with a group whose leader allegedly had "served as a sponsor or endorser of a number of Communist-front activities."

The *New York Times* article suggested that Kitt might have been the target of such a detailed investigation on account of remarks she made during a White House luncheon in January, 1968. At that event, Kitt shouted that the nation's young people were rebelling because they were being "snatched off to be shot in Vietnam." Both President and Mrs. Lyndon Johnson were reportedly upset by the singer's outburst.

Kitt responded to the reports by declaring, "I don't understand this at all. I think it's disgusting.... I've always lived a very clean life and I have nothing to be afraid of and I have nothing to hide."

In another case, the *Washington Post* reported on January 25 that the FBI had wiretapped the conversations of Martin Luther King, Jr., and other civil rights leaders during the 1964 Democratic National Convention in Atlantic City, New Jersey. According to the newspaper, the reports from the wiretaps were delivered to President Lyndon Johnson. (Also see entries dated March 28, 1975, and June 6, 1975.)

January 8. Students returned to school in South Boston, Massachusetts, for the first time in four weeks as more than 400 police officers kept watch on the arrival and departure of school buses. Four schools in the area had been closed since December 11, 1974, when a white student was stabbed at South Boston High School. (Also see entries dated September 12-October 31, 1974, and January 21-May 31, 1976.)

January 12-15. Celebrations were held throughout the nation commemorating the forty-sixth birthday of slain civil rights leader Martin Luther King, Jr. Much of the activity was focused in King's hometown of Atlanta, Georgia.

On January 15, an ecumenical service was held at the Ebenezer Baptist Church where King had served as pastor. Other activities in King's hometown during the day included the dedication of the civil rights leader's birthplace as a national historic site and a "people's march" in the downtown area of the city.

January 15. John Lewis, executive director of the Voter Education Project (VEP), was awarded the Martin Luther King, Jr., Non-violent Peace Prize for 1975. The award is the highest prize given by the Martin Luther King, Jr., Center for Social Change.

Lewis began his civil rights career as a member of the Student Non-Violent Coordinating Committee (SNCC). Later, he served as the group's executive director. He participated in the first Freedom Rides in 1961 and was a principal speaker at the March on Washington in 1963. Lewis was also a leader of the Selma-to-Montgomery voting rights marches during the mid-1960s.

January 24. J. Mason Brewer, possibly the best known writer of African American folklore in the United States, died in Commerce, Texas, at the age of seventy-eight.

Brewer wrote some of his stories and poems in black dialect that was so old most people had trouble reading it. Others he wrote in standard English. The late J. Frank Dobie, himself a distinguished folklorist, once called Brewer "the best storyteller of Negro folklore anywhere in the world."

February 25. Elijah Muhammad, leader of the Black Muslims, died in Chicago, Illinois, at the age of seventy-seven.

During the height of the civil rights movement, Muhammad and his followers angered whites as well as blacks for preaching racial separatism, racial pride, and self-defense. (See entry dated July 31, 1960.) But upon his death, many who had once disagreed with him stepped forward to praise the man whose teachings had become increasingly popular among blacks. Jesse Jackson, for example, praised Muhammad as "the single most powerful black man in this country.... His leadership extended far beyond his membership. He was the father of black self-consciousness during our 'colored' and Negro days."

Muhammad was succeeded by his son, Wallace D. Muhammad. (Also see entries dated November, 1934, and March 12, 1964.)

February 28. In Memphis, Tennessee, U.S. District Court Judge Robert M. McRae, Jr., denied James Earl Ray's motion to withdraw his guilty plea and face a new trial on the charge that he murdered Dr. Martin Luther King, Jr., in 1968. McRae said Ray's original plea of guilty was "coolly and deliberately" submitted and that he found no grounds for a retrial. Robert Livingston, one of Ray's new attorneys, announced he would immediately file an appeal with the U.S. Court of Appeals for the Sixth Circuit. (Also see entries dated April 4, 1968; March 10, 1969; January 8, 1970; June 21, 1974; June 29, 1974; and October 29, 1974.)

March 24. Heavyweight boxing champion Muhammad Ali defeated Chuck Wepner in the final round of a fifteen-round title fight to retain his crown.

March 28. The *Washington Star* reported new evidence of governmental spying on black individuals and organizations.

These included investigations of Marion Barry, a former SNCC activist and ex-president of the Board of Education of Washington, D.C.; Walter Fauntroy, the District of Columbia's delegate to the U.S. House of Representatives; David Eaton, pastor of Washington's All Souls Unitarian Church; and Absalom Frederick Jordan, chairman of the Black United Front. (Also see entries dated January 2-26, 1975, and June 6, 1975.)

April 1. The Black Christian Nationalist (BCN) Church opened its Third Biennial National Convention in Atlanta, Georgia.

Headed by Jaramazi Abebe Agyeman (formerly Albert Cleage), the BCN was a movement dedicated to changing the condition of black people by changing their lifestyles. According to the creed of the BCN, "Jesus, the Black Messiah, was a revolutionary leader, sent by God to rebuild the Black Nation, Israel, and to liberate Black people from powerlessness and from the oppression, brutality and exploitation of the white gentile world."

April 8. One of the last remaining barriers in professional sports fell as Lee Elder, a black golfer, began competing in the preliminary rounds of the famed Masters Tournament at Augusta, Georgia. He failed to make the cut, however, and therefore did not play in the actual tournament.

April 12. Josephine Baker, one of the most popular American singers in France since the 1920s, died in Paris at the age of sixty-nine.

Baker began dancing and singing as a small child. She was only fifteen when she left her hometown of St. Louis, Missouri, with a traveling dance troupe. She soon ended up in New York City, where she began performing regularly at the Radio City Music Hall and the Plantation Club in Harlem.

In 1925, after Broadway rejected her as "too ugly," Baker went to Paris. There she became an instant success in the all-black *Blackbird Revue,* which introduced jazz to eager French audiences. During the 1920s and 1930s, Baker starred in shows of her own at the Folies-Bergeres and the Casino de Paris that made her wildly popular. Audiences loved her sultry voice and sexy dance moves. She lived the life of a true celebrity and, in 1937, she became a French citizen.

Josephine Baker

During the Second World War, Baker volunteered her services to the Red Cross. She also worked for the French underground, a secret network of people who took action against the Nazis. After the war, in gratitude for her willingness to take on dangerous assignments, the French government awarded her the Croix de Guerre, the Legion of Honor, and the Resistance Medal.

Baker returned to the world of entertainment in the late 1940s. But during the 1950s, she began to devote more and more of her time and energy to the home she had set up in the French countryside for orphaned children of all races and nationalities. Within just a few years, however, she had used up most of her fortune. So she spent the rest of her life periodically returning to the stage to earn a little more money for what she called her "rainbow family."

In April, 1975, Baker celebrated the 50th anniversary of her first appearance in Paris with a gala performance of a show entitled *Josephine.* Two days later, she collapsed and died just before going onstage.

April 14. In the Superior Court of Beaufort County, North Carolina, the highly publicized murder case of a twenty-year-old black woman named Joann Little got under way.

In August, 1974, Little was being held in the Beaufort County Jail on charges of breaking and entering. But after a jail guard, Clarence Alligood, was found stabbed to death in her cell on August 27, the young woman suddenly found herself facing a murder charge. She claimed it was a case of self-defense because the guard had tried to rape her.

The case began to attract national attention after civil rights groups and feminist organizations came to Little's defense. They argued that her experience was typical of the kind of abuse that blacks and women have suffered for a long time in the southern criminal justice system. Her attorneys insisted that racist feelings and widespread publicity had made it impossible for her to get a fair trial in Beaufort County.

By early April, Little's supporters had raised thousands of dollars to defend her. Also, Representative Shirley Chisholm from New York had asked U.S. Attorney General Edward Levy to intervene in the case on Little's behalf. As Representative Chisholm said: "There are very few black people of either sex called to serve on juries in these eastern North Carolina counties. So this can really hurt Joann, who lives in a region where many, many Caucasian people hold the worst sort of prejudices against black women." (Also see entry dated August 15, 1975.)

April 23. Racial fighting erupted at the Boca Raton High School in Boca Raton, Florida, a wealthy resort community.

Police said the clash began about 7:00 a.m. when several buses carrying black students from Delray Beach arrived at the school. The blacks spotted a racial slur written on the wall and became angry, and the fight was soon on. Three students and a police officer were injured. Two white students were arrested on charges of disorderly conduct.

June 6. New reports of FBI spying on black individuals and organizations appeared in the *Atlanta Constitution.*

According to the newspaper, the FBI had spied on the Afro-American Patrolmen's League since its founding in Chicago, Illinois, in 1968. (The Afro-American's Patrolmen's League was organized to give a voice to black police officers with racial complaints.) The founder of the Patrolmen's League, Renault Robinson, claimed that the FBI shared its information with Army intelligence units and with the intelligence division of the Chicago Police Department. (Also see entries dated January 2-26, 1975, and March 28, 1975.)

July 5. In England, African American tennis star Arthur Ashe beat top-ranked Jimmy Connors to become the first black to win the men's singles title at the prestigious Wimbledon tournament.

A native of Richmond, Virginia, Ashe was born in 1943. He first played tennis when he was only seven years old, using a borrowed racket and practicing with it on the segregated courts near his home. Noticing that Ashe had talent, a playground instructor arranged for him to spend some time with Robert W. Johnson, a doctor from Lynchburg, Virginia, who had made a second career out of training promising young black tennis players. (Althea Gibson had once been his student.)

Arthur Ashe

Over the course of several summers, Johnson helped Ashe work on his game. He also taught the youngster how to handle the pressures of competition without showing anger or frustration. Years later, Ashe put those lessons to the test time and time again. On the court, he displayed a sense of dignity, quiet determination, and an almost "superhuman calmness" that amazed—and sometimes annoyed—his opponents. As the only black in a sport dominated by wealthy whites, he changed people's ideas about black athletes.

Ashe's rise up the amateur ranks continued throughout the 1960s. In 1963, for example, he was the first black named to the U.S. Davis Cup team. At the time, he was attending the University of California at Los Angeles (UCLA) on a tennis scholarship, training under Pancho Gonzalez and J.D. Morgan. After graduating in

1966, Ashe served briefly in the U.S. Army and played tennis whenever he could. In 1968, he became the first black male to win top honors at the U.S. Open Championship in Forest Hills, New York. The following year, after his army service ended, he turned professional and began to devote himself completely to tennis.

Throughout the 1970s, Ashe racked up a series of important victories (such as the Australian Open and the French Open), including the one at Wimbledon. But the decade ended on a frightening note. In 1979, he suffered a heart attack that forced him to retire from the game in 1980 after undergoing bypass surgery.

Ashe then turned his attention to other matters. Always a "quiet warrior" in the battle against racial discrimination, he stepped up his campaign against South African apartheid. He also spoke out about the unfair treatment of athletes (especially black athletes) and cofounded a special players' union, the Association of Tennis Professionals.

Ashe tackled many other jobs, too, working as a sports commentator, host of his own television program, newspaper and magazine columnist, and author, to name only a few. (In 1988, he published a history of the black athlete in America entitled *A Hard Road to Glory*.) In addition, he was active on behalf of several charities, especially the American Heart Association and the Children's Defense Fund. He remained involved in tennis as captain of the U.S. Davis Cup team from 1981 until 1985 and as a promoter of and instructor at tennis clinics for inner-city youths. (Also see entries dated April 7, 1992, and February 6, 1993.)

July 24-28. On July 24, the U.S. Senate agreed to extend the Voting Rights Act of 1965 for an additional seven years. On July 28, the U.S. House of Representatives approved the same measure.

The original Voting Rights Act of 1965 had allowed federal registrars and the Department of Justice to help thousands of blacks to register and vote in the South. (See entry dated May 26, 1965.) In the past, politicians from the region had tried to block passage of the act. This time around, however, it was supported by a few southern senators and dozens of representatives. Some of them had failed earlier in an attempt to extend the coverage of the law from the South to the entire nation.

August 6-15. Racial violence continued in Boston, Massachusetts, the scene of sporadic incidents ever since the city began busing students to achieve school desegregation.

On August 6, racial fighting erupted at the Charles Street Jail. On August 10, black and white swimmers threw rocks and bricks at one another on South Boston's Carson Beach. On August 13, police stepped up their patrols in the predominantly black Roxbury section of the city, where young blacks had been attacking white passersby on and off for three days. And on August 15, three people were slightly injured during incidents of stone throwing in the city. Meanwhile, the state's black U.S. senator, Edward Brooke, joined local leaders in an attempt to ease racial tensions.

August 8. Julian "Cannonball" Adderley, once described as a "prophet of contemporary jazz," died in Gary, Indiana. Known primarily as an alto saxophonist, Adderley also played tenor sax, trumpet, clarinet, and flute.

Adderley was born in Tampa, Florida, in 1928, the son of a jazz cornetist. He studied brass and reed instruments in a Tallahassee, Florida, high school, where he formed his first jazz group. Because of his hearty appetite, fellow students nicknamed him "Cannibal," which later became "Cannonball."

From 1948 until 1956, Adderley was music director at Dillard High School in Fort Lauderdale, Florida. At the same time, he directed his own jazz group in southern Florida. He then served for three years as a member of the 36th Army Dance Band and later studied at the Naval School of Music in Washington, D.C.

Adderley's first big break came in New York City in 1955 when he appeared with noted jazz bassist Oscar Pettiford. The next year he signed his first recording contract with EmArcy Records, and he was on his way.

Until 1957, Adderley toured with his brother, Nat, a cornetist. In 1957, he joined the Miles Davis group. In 1959, after a tour with George Shearing, Adderley formed his own quintet, which again included his brother Nat. That same year, *Down Beat* magazine named him its New Alto Star of the Year.

Among Adderley's best-known recordings are the albums *Black Messiah, Country Preacher, Fiddler on the Roof, Walk Tall,* and *Quiet Nights.* His last album was *Phoenix.*

August 15. A jury of six whites and six blacks in Raleigh, North Carolina, found Joann Little, a black woman, not guilty of the murder of white jail guard Clarence Alligood. (Also see entry dated April 14, 1975.)

September 1. Lieutenant General Daniel "Chappie" James, Jr., became the first African American to be promoted to the rank of four star general in the U.S. Armed Forces. A veteran of nearly 200 combat missions in Korea and Vietnam, the fifty-five-year-old James was also made chief of the North American Air Defense Command (NORAD). His appointment brought the number of black generals and admirals in the Army, Air Force, and Navy to twenty-one (out of a total of about 1,200).

James was born and raised in Pensacola, Florida, during a period of rigid racial segregation. His mother, Lillie A. James, who founded her own school for black youths, encouraged him to dream of higher things. He went on to graduate from Tuskegee Institute and became one of the original black pilots in the U.S. Army Air Corps, the forerunner of today's Air Force.

Commenting on his mother's influence, James once stated: "My mother used to say, 'Don't stand there banging on the door of opportunity, then, when someone opens it, you say, "Wait a minute, I got to get my bags." You be prepared with your bags of knowledge, your patriotism, your honor, and when somebody opens that door, you charge in.'" (Also see entry dated February 25, 1978.)

November 19. James B. Adams, associate deputy director of the FBI, told the U.S. Senate's Intelligence Committee that there was no legal justification for the Bureau's attempts during the 1960s to discredit the late Dr. Martin Luther King, Jr., as a civil rights leader.

Adams said the FBI investigated King because of the possibility that Communists were influencing him as well as the civil rights movement. No such evidence was ever uncovered, however. (Also see entries dated May 29-June 3, 1978, and November 17, 1978.)

November 19. Accompanied by federal officers, former Black Panther Party leader Eldridge Cleaver arrived in California to face charges of attempted murder.

Cleaver was being held in connection with a 1968 shootout between the Panthers and police in Oakland, California. During the incident, seventeen-year-old Panther Bobby Hutton was killed and a police officer was wounded. Cleaver later jumped bail and fled overseas. He lived in Cuba, Guinea, Algeria, North Korea, and France during his seven years in exile. He finally returned on his own to the United States because he thought the country "had changed" enough for him to get a fair trial.

In exchange for Cleaver's guilty plea in an assault case involving an Oakland policeman, a California court dropped the 1968 murder charge against him. He was then sentenced to probation and ordered to perform 2,000 hours of community service.

Not long after his return, Cleaver announced that his seven years in exile had made him look at the world differently—he had become a conservative, "born-again" Christian. Since then, Cleaver has toured the country as an evangelist. (Also see entry dated April 6, 1968.)

November 21. John Calhoun, a former Foreign Service Officer and deputy special assistant to President Gerald Ford, was appointed special assistant to the president for Minority Affairs. At the time of his new appointment, Calhoun had been a member of the White House staff since 1973.

1976

January 21-May 31. More racial violence erupted in Boston, Massachusetts, during protests by whites against court-ordered school desegregation.

On January 21, black and white students at Hyde Park High School fought with fists and chairs. Across the city in East Boston, approximately 300 whites tried to block a major Boston Harbor tunnel during the morning rush hour. On February 15, about 2,000 people fought the police near South Boston High School, the center of the fiercest opposition to school desegregation. On May 30, a fire was set next to the replica of the *Beaver,* a two-masted sailing ship that was moored at a bridge that leads into South Boston. (Also see entries dated September 12-October 31, 1974, and January 8, 1975.)

January 23. Actor, singer, and civil rights activist Paul Robeson died in Philadelphia, Pennsylvania, at the age of seventy-seven.

Robeson was born on April 9, 1898, in Princeton, New Jersey. An outstanding scholar and athlete, he graduated from Rutgers University with honors in 1919.

Robeson then went on to law school. But the racial prejudice he experienced when he accepted his first job in the legal profession quickly left him angry and frustrated, and he soon quit. At the urging of his wife, Eslanda, Robeson then reluctantly agreed to try out his rich baritone voice on the stage as a singer and actor. In 1920, he won a role in a play at the Harlem YMCA. "Even then," Robeson later recalled, "I never meant to [become an actor]. I just said yes to get her to quit pestering me."

Paul Robeson

The Harlem performance, however, launched his stage career. In 1922, he made his first Broadway appearance in a play called *Taboo*. (Later that year he made his London debut in the same play, which had been retitled *The Voodoo*.) After returning to New York in late 1922, Robeson joined the Provincetown Players, a Greenwich Village group that included dramatist Eugene O'Neill. He then appeared in O'Neill's *All God's Chillun Got Wings*. This led to a successful appearance in the lead role of another O'Neill work, *The Emperor Jones*. He followed that with triumphant performances in London productions of *The Emperor Jones* as well as the musical *Show Boat*. (It featured the song "Ol' Man River," which became identified with Robeson for the rest of his life.) Heading back to New York, he then appeared on Broadway in George Gershwin's *Porgy and Bess*.

Robeson's successes during this period were not limited to acting, however. In 1925, the Provincetown Players sponsored his first major concert. Robeson pulled together a program that focused on black spirituals and folk songs. It was a big hit with New York audiences, and soon Robeson found himself on a singing tour of Great Britain and Europe that brought him even greater acclaim.

To escape racial prejudice in the United States, Robeson lived overseas most of the time between 1928 and 1939. He spent much of his time in London, where he enjoyed one of his greatest stage triumphs—playing the lead in a 1930 production of William Shakespeare's *Othello*. He followed it with another tour of the major cities of Europe both as a recitalist and an actor.

It was during his stay in Europe that Robeson became increasingly interested in politics and social issues, especially as they related to economics and racism. In 1934, he visited the Soviet Union for the first time and was very impressed by the apparent lack of racial prejudice among the Soviet people. Soon Robeson began publicly expressing his support for Soviet-style socialism. He then became a full-fledged activist on behalf of antifascist causes, African national liberation movements, and various labor groups.

In 1939, with Europe on the verge of war, Robeson returned to the United States. Over the next few years he continued to enjoy tremendous success as a performer. On October 19, 1943, for example, Robeson became the first black actor to play the title role of *Othello* (with a white supporting cast) before a Broadway audience. The next year, the NAACP gave him its highest award, the Spingarn Medal.

Meanwhile, Robeson became increasingly active politically. But his harsh criticism of American racism and economic policy was often accompanied by extravagant praise for the Soviets. This led some people—even his biggest fans—to question his loyalty to his country. Eventually, his words and actions caused enough of an uproar that his popularity declined sharply.

Throughout the late 1940s and well into the 1950s, Robeson was called before congressional committees on several occasions to answer questions about his activities and beliefs. In 1950, the U.S. State Department canceled his passport because he refused to sign a statement swearing that he was not a Communist. Robeson then sued the State Department. He regained his passport in 1958 as a result of a U.S. Supreme Court decision in a similar case.

Once Robeson was free to travel overseas again, he left immediately for Great Britain, where he was still popular. He continued to tour around the world for several years until poor health forced him to retire from the stage. In 1963, he and his wife returned to the United States to live quietly in a Harlem apartment. Two years later, after his wife's death, Robeson moved to Philadelphia, Pennsylvania, to live with his sister. There he spent his remaining years completely out of the public eye.

Despite his difficulties with Congress, the State Department, and many American organizations and individuals, Robeson was a hero to much of black America and to countless other people throughout the world. As Prime Minister Jawaharlal Nehru of India observed at a celebration of Robeson's sixtieth birthday in 1958: "[He is] one of the greatest artists of our generation [who] reminds us that art and human dignity are above differences of race, nationality, and color."

January 28. Vivian W. Henderson, president of Clark College in Georgia, died during heart surgery in Atlanta at the age of fifty-two.

Henderson, a native of Bristol, Virginia, was born on February 10, 1923. He received a bachelor's degree from North Carolina College in Durham (later North Carolina Central University) and earned master's and doctorate degrees in economics from the University of Iowa.

In 1948, Henderson began his teaching career in Texas at Prairie View A & M College. He then returned to North Carolina College the following year as a professor of economics. In 1952, Henderson moved to a similar position at Fisk University in Tennessee, where he eventually became chairman of the Department of Economics. He was named president of Clark College in 1965.

In addition to his roles as a teacher and an administrator, Henderson achieved distinction as one of the nation's leading African American scholars in economics. He was the author of *The Economic Status of Negroes* (1963), co-author of *The Advancing South: Manpower Prospects and Problems* (1959), and contributing author of *Principles of Economics* (1959). He also contributed to *Race, Regions and Jobs,* edited by Arthur Ross and Herbert Hill in 1967. According to the *Atlanta Journal,* his work "is considered to have had an important impact in convincing industry and business of the buying power of the black American community."

February 5-26. Racial violence erupted in Pensacola, Florida, over the issue of whether athletic teams at a local high school would be called "Rebels" or "Raiders."

On February 5, 1,500 people rioted at the Escambia High School. Four white students were wounded by gunfire and six others were injured. At least nine people were arrested, including a twenty-three-year-old black man who was a suspect in the shootings.

Over the next few weeks, crosses were burned on the lawns of school board members and a bullet was fired through the window of a black school board member. In addition, arsonists set fire to the homes of a local human relations council member and a state representative who had both been involved in the "Rebels" versus "Raiders" controversy. Blacks responded by boycotting the school.

The trouble dated back to 1973, when black students first objected to the "Rebels" nickname and the flying of the Confederate flag at athletic events and other functions. They said both symbols were a direct insult to them. After several protests, some of which turned violent, a U.S. District Court permanently banned the use of the rebel name, the flag, "and related symbols on the grounds that they were 'racially irritating.'" Students then chose the name "Raiders" to represent the school.

But after an appeal by a group of white students and school board members, a U.S. Court of Appeals overturned the District Court ruling and told school board members to decide the matter. They scheduled another student vote for February 4, 1976, and the riot erupted the next day.

March 20. Former middleweight boxer Rubin "Hurricane" Carter and another man, John Artis, were released from prison in New Jersey after serving nine years for murder.

The two black men, who were casual friends, had been convicted in 1967 for allegedly participating in the fatal shootings of three people in a bar in Patterson, New Jersey, on June 17, 1966. The shootings occurred at a time of heightened racial tensions in the city. Two ex-convicts had testified that they saw Carter and Artis at the murder scene with guns. But the defendants insisted they were not guilty of the crime. Many blacks believed the two men were being prosecuted and persecuted because of their race. A number of celebrities, including boxer Muhammad Ali and singer Bob Dylan, attracted national attention to the case with their support of the effort to win new trials for Carter and Artis.

In September, 1974, the *New York Times* reported that the ex-convicts had taken back what they had said on the witness stand, claiming that police detectives had pressured them to lie. On March 17, 1976, the Supreme Court of New Jersey agreed and reversed the convictions of Carter and Artis. Three days later, both were set free on bond pending new trials.

June 25. The U.S. Supreme Court voted to ban private schools from excluding blacks on the basis of their race.

June 25. The U.S. Supreme Court ruled unanimously that victims of so-called reverse discrimination have the same rights as blacks to sue in federal courts if they have been fired from their jobs. The Court said that the Civil Rights Act of 1964 was "not limited to discrimination against members of any particular race." (Also see entries dated June 28, 1978; June 12, 1984; January 23, 1989; and June 12, 1989.)

July 15. Jimmy Carter, former governor of Georgia, accepted the Democratic nomination for president of the United States at the close of his party's national convention in New York City.

September 19. William "Bill" Lucas, a former baseball player for the Milwaukee and Atlanta Braves of the National Baseball League, was named director of player personnel for the Braves. At the time, it was the highest position ever held by an African American in professional baseball.

Lucas had joined the Braves' executive staff after leaving the playing field in 1964, first in sales and promotions and then in public relations. He also served as assistant farm director and director of player development.

September 28. In New York City, Muhammad Ali won a hard-fought bout against challenger Ken Norton to retain his world heavyweight championship title.

October 4. President Gerald Ford accepted the resignation of Secretary of Agriculture Earl Butz. In a private conversation following the Republican National Convention in August, 1976, Butz had accused blacks of being lazy and shiftless. The slurs had been traced back to him in September.

October 25. Alabama governor George Wallace pardoned sixty-four-year-old Clarence "Willie" Norris, "the last of 'the Scottsboro Boys,'" for a 1931 rape conviction.

Norris was one of eight young black men convicted of raping two white women near Scottsboro, Alabama, and sentenced to death. The U.S. Supreme Court later overturned the conviction. After one of the alleged victims recanted, or took back, what she had said about the rape, the court set aside a guilty verdict in a second trial. The eight men were then convicted at a third trial. By that time, however, everyone but Norris, who escaped while on parole in 1946, had already been pardoned.

The NAACP, along with the Communist Party and other groups, had protested and taken legal action on behalf of the "Scottsboro Boys" for over twenty years. When

Norris was finally pardoned, the NAACP announced it was taking that to mean he had been completely cleared of any wrongdoing and that this applied to the other men as well. All of the other "Scottsboro Boys," however, were believed to be dead at the time of Norris's pardon. (Also see entry dated April 6, 1931.)

November 2. Democrat Jimmy Carter, the former governor of Georgia, narrowly defeated Republican Gerald Ford to become the new president of the United States. (Ford had led the country since August, 1974, after the Watergate scandal forced President Richard Nixon to resign.) Black voters had overwhelmingly supported Carter in his campaign for the nation's highest office.

December 16. President-elect Jimmy Carter announced the nomination of Georgia congressman Andrew Young as U.S. Ambassador to the United Nations, a cabinet-level position. It was the first time an African American had ever been asked to lead the American delegation at the world peace organization. (Also see entry dated January 30, 1977.)

December 23. President-elect Jimmy Carter named a second black to his cabinet he chose District of Columbia attorney Patricia Roberts Harris as Secretary of Housing and Urban Development (HUD).

1977   **January 19.** President-elect Jimmy Carter named black attorney Clifford Alexander, Jr., to the position of Secretary of the Army. It was the first time in U.S. history that an African American had been chosen to serve in that post.

January 27. U.S. Attorney General Griffin Bell selected Drew Days, a thirty-six-year-old black lawyer, to be assistant attorney general in charge of civil rights in the U.S. Department of Justice. The appointment made history in two ways—Days was the country's first black assistant attorney general and also the first black person ever to oversee civil rights enforcement.

January 30. Andrew Young, an African American congressman from Georgia, took the oath of office as U.S. Ambassador to the United Nations (UN), the highest diplomatic post ever held by a black American. The appointment also carried cabinet rank in the administration of President Jimmy Carter.

Young was born in New Orleans, Louisiana, on March 12, 1932. He received a bachelor's degree from Howard University in 1951 and a Bachelor of Divinity degree at the Hartford Theological Seminary in Connecticut in 1951. He was then ordained a minister in the United Church of Christ. His early assignments were at churches in Marion, Alabama, and the Georgia towns of Thomasville and Beachton.

After a brief period of service with the National Council of Churches, Young joined the staff of the Southern Christian Leadership Conference (SCLC). In 1964, Martin Luther King, Jr., named him executive director of the SCLC, and in 1967 he became its executive vice-president.

Young entered national politics in 1970 when he ran unsuccessfully for Congress from Georgia's Fifth District. Two years later, after the majority white district had been redivided, he was then elected as the first black Georgia congressman since the Reconstruction era. The voters returned him to Congress in 1974 and again in 1976.

February 3. The "Roots" miniseries, based on Alex Haley's novel of the same title in which he traced his ancestry from the time of slavery back to his tribal beginnings in Africa, ended its spectacularly successful run on the ABC television network. The final episode on Sunday evening received the highest single ratings of any program in television history. (The previous record-holder was the epic Civil War movie, *Gone with the Wind*.) More than 130 million people watched the eight-part drama. (Also see entries dated September 11, 1977, and February 10, 1992.)

Alex Haley (right) with a Gambian government official

March 9. A group of armed Black Muslims took hostages at three sites in Washington,

D.C.—the offices of the Jewish organization B'nai B'rith, an Islamic center, and the Washington city hall. At city hall, Maurice Williams, a twenty-two-year-old radio reporter, was killed and at least eleven others were wounded. Washington's mayor Walter Washington barricaded himself inside his office.

The gunmen demanded that the premiere of the film *Mohammad, Messenger of God* be canceled because they said it "ridiculed the Prophet." Another gunman, however, said the attacks were in revenge for the 1973 slayings in Washington of seven Hanafi Muslims. The Hanafis were allegedly killed by members of a rival Muslim sect.

April 14. William H. Hastie, the first black person appointed to a U.S. Court of Appeals, died after collapsing on a golf course in Philadelphia, Pennsylvania. He was seventy-one.

Hastie began serving on the U.S. Court of Appeals for the Third Circuit in 1949. He retired from the court as chief judge in 1971. (Also see entries dated March 26, 1937; May 1, 1946; and October 15, 1949.)

May 16. In Landover, Maryland, Muhammad Ali retained his world heavyweight boxing championship with a unanimous decision over twenty-two-year-old Alfredo Evangelista of Uruguay after a fifteen-round fight.

August 1. Ethel Waters, African American singer and actress, died of apparent heart failure in Chatsworth, California, at the age of seventy-six.

Waters was born on October 31, 1900, in Chester, Pennsylvania. She first appeared on stage at age seventeen and later toured with jazz and blues groups, becoming a well-known entertainer on the nightclub and vaudeville circuit. (She was reportedly the first woman to sing W.C. Handy's "St. Louis Blues" on stage.) But after a religious conversion, Waters gave up performing in such nightspots.

Waters made her Broadway debut in *Plantation Revue of 1924*. In this production, she scored one of the greatest song hits ever when she introduced the piece "Dinah." She then began appearing in movies, including *As Thousands Cheer, At Home Abroad,* and *Rhapsody in Black*. In the early 1940s, she starred on both stage and screen in *Cabin in the Sky*. Waters followed this triumph with roles in such films as *Pinky,* for which she received an Academy Award nomination. She gave another memorable performance in the 1950 play *Member of the Wedding* as well as its 1953 movie version. Waters's last film was *The Sound and the Fury* in 1958. She then turned to television and made appearances on programs such as "The Tennessee Ernie Ford Show," "Daniel Boone," and "Route 66."

Later in her life, Waters devoted more and more of her time to singing, becoming famous for blues renditions of "Am I Blue" and "Stormy Weather" as well as Negro spirituals. She sang with the Billy Graham Crusade for fifteen years, thrilling millions around the world with her rendition of "His Eye Is on the Sparrow," a song from *Member of the Wedding*. Waters's autobiography, also entitled *His Eye Is on the Sparrow,* was published in 1951 and became a bestseller.

During the 1960s, Waters grew increasingly ill with diabetes and heart problems. By this time she had also lost much of her wealth and was just getting by on Social Security. Offered a chance to make money doing television commercials, she refused. Despite facing hard times, Waters declared, "I couldn't be happier because I'm at peace with the Lord."

September 11. The epic television miniseries "Roots," based on Alex Haley's novel of the same name, swept the Nineteenth Annual Emmy Award presentations in Los Angeles, California.

Among the winners connected with the miniseries were Lou Gossett, Jr., who was named outstanding lead actor, and Edward Asner and Olivia Cole, who were recognized for their supporting roles. Writers Ernest Kinoy and William Blinn and director David Greene also received Emmys. In addition, the drama also won the award as Outstanding Limited Series. (Also see entries dated February 3, 1977, and February 10, 1992.)

October 3. Ten members of the U.S. House of Representatives signed a declaration calling for the impeachment of Andrew Young, the first African American ambassador to the United Nations (UN).

Young had angered some people with various public statements he made both before and after he became ambassador to the UN. (For example, he had described Great Britain and Sweden as racist nations.) The resolution also accused Young of failing to oppose the admission of Vietnam to the United Nations and of trying to "transfer the governing power in the anti-communist nation of Rhodesia to the pro-Marxist guerilla coalition." (Also see entries dated January 30, 1977, and August 15, 1979.)

Reggie Jackson

October 18. Reggie Jackson, African American outfielder for the New York Yankees of the American Baseball League, hit three home runs in a single World Series game. It was the first time in history that anyone had accomplished such a feat. Dodgers manager Tommy Lasorda called Jackson's achievement "the greatest performance that I've ever seen in a World Series."

The Yankees went on to defeat the National League's Los Angeles Dodgers to capture the 1977 World Series title.

October 29. In New York City, Muhammad Ali retained the world heavyweight boxing championship with a unanimous, fifteen-round decision over challenger Earnie Shavers.

November 18. Robert Edward Chambliss, a seventy-three-year-old former Ku Klux Klansman, was convicted of first degree murder in the 1963 dynamite bombing of the Sixteenth Street Baptist Church in Birmingham, Alabama. The blast killed four young black girls who had been attending Sunday School. (See entry dated September 15, 1963.)

A lack of evidence had led to the fourteen-year delay in bringing Chambliss to justice for one of the most tragic and shameful crimes of the civil rights era. He had been arrested shortly after the bombing for possession of dynamite, but further investigations by local and state authorities as well as the FBI did not uncover enough information to bring other charges against him. In 1975, however, Alabama's attorney general took a closer look at the old files and launched a new investigation into the bombing. His efforts eventually resulted in Chambliss' arrest for murder. He was convicted specifically for the death of eleven-year-old Carol Denise McNair. He was immediately sentenced to a term of life in prison.

December 10. Barbara Jordan, African American congresswoman from Texas, announced that she would not seek reelection. She denied rumors of poor health and also said she would not seek a seat on the federal bench. She did say, however, that "the longer you stay in Congress, the harder it is to leave.... I didn't want to wake up one fine sunny morning and say there is nothing else to do."

Born February 21, 1936, in Houston, Texas, Jordan studied government at Texas Southern University, where she also was a standout member of the school's debate team. She earned a law degree at Boston University in 1959, then returned to Texas to open a private law practice. During this same period, Jordan also became politically active as a volunteer for John F. Kennedy and Lyndon B. Johnson in the 1960 presidential election.

Her first try at running for office came in 1962, when she lost a bid to become a member of the Texas House of Representatives. She tried again in 1964 and lost a second time. But in 1966, she aimed for a seat in the Texas State Senate. Her victory in that election made her the first woman ever elected to the Texas State Senate and the state's first black senator since 1883.

After six successful years in office, Jordan ran for the U.S. House of Representatives and won. She arrived in Washington in January, 1973, to take her seat in Congress on behalf of Houston's Eighteenth District.

Barbara Jordan

During the impeachment hearings for President Richard Nixon in 1974, Jordan captured national attention with an eloquent condemnation of the president's involvement in the Watergate burglary scandal and an equally eloquent defense of the U.S. Constitution. Two years later at the Democratic National Convention in New York City, she once again electrified a nationwide audience with a speech in which she described her vision of a government that involves all its citizens.

After retiring from Congress, Jordan accepted a teaching position at the University of Texas at Austin in the Lyndon B. Johnson School of Public Affairs. In addition to teaching, she is a faculty advisor and a minority recruiter. More recently, Jordan has also served Governor Ann Richards of Texas as an advisor on ethics in government.

1978   **January 15.** Walter Payton, African American running back for the Chicago Bears, was named the National Football League's Most Valuable Player for 1977.

A graduate of Jackson State University in Mississippi, Payton led the League in rushing with 1,852 yards during the 1977 season, his third year in the NFL (a league record). In a game against the Minnesota Vikings on November 20, he ran for 275 yards, breaking a record set by African American O.J. Simpson. Payton also beat Simpson's record of 332 carries with 339 of his own. Finally, Payton's 1,852 total yards rushing during the season was third only to Simpson's 2,003 and the African American Jim Brown's 1,863.

February 15. Twenty-four-year-old Leon Spinks, a black former Marine, defeated thirty-six-year-old Muhammad Ali for the heavyweight boxing championship of the world. The championship was given to Spinks after fifteen rounds on a split decision by ring officials. Both men were former Olympic light heavyweight champions—Ali in 1960 in Rome, Italy, and Spinks in 1976 in Montreal, Canada.

Spinks's victory represented one of the biggest upsets in world heavyweight title history since Ali himself beat the late Sonny Liston in 1964.

February 25. Daniel "Chappie" James, Jr., the only four-star black general in the U.S. Armed Forces, died of a heart attack in Colorado Springs, Colorado, at the age of fifty-eight.

James had gone from pushing a coal cart in a Pensacola, Florida, gas plant to serving as one of the nation's most influential military leaders. Before retiring from the military on January 26, 1978, he had also gained fame for his speeches on Americanism and patriotism. As he once wrote on a portrait of himself that hangs in the Pentagon: "I fought three wars and three more wouldn't be too many to defend my country.... I love America and as she has weaknesses or ills, I'll hold her hand." (Also see entry dated September 1, 1975.)

March 24. Bill Kenny, "whose tenor voice helped make the original Ink Spots one of the world's best known singing groups in the 1940s," died of a respiratory ailment in New Westminster, British Columbia, Canada, at the age of sixty-three.

Together with Charles Fuqua, Orville Jones, and Ivory Watson, Kenny formed the Ink Spots in 1939. He was the last survivor of the group and continued performing and recording almost up until his death.

April 17. James Alan McPherson, Jr., an African American author, was awarded a Pulitzer Prize in fiction for *Elbow Room,* a volume of short stories on the black experience.

A thirty-four-year-old native of Savannah, Georgia, McPherson received a bachelor's degree from Morris Brown College in 1965 and a law degree from Harvard University in 1968. A year later he earned a master of fine arts degree from the University of Iowa.

Since then, McPherson has taught English, literature, and writing at several different schools, including the University of Iowa. He has also served as a contributing editor of *Atlantic Monthly* magazine and a contributor to *Black Insights, Cutting Edges,* and *New Black Voices.* Among McPherson's other writings are *Hue and Cry,* a collection of short stories published in 1969, and *Railroad: Trains and Train People in American Culture,* an anthology he edited in 1976.

May 29-June 3. On May 29, Joseph Lowery, president of the Southern Christian Leadership Conference (SCLC) urged the FBI to release "all the facts" in the Bureau's "attempt to discredit Dr. Martin Luther King, Jr. during the 1960s."

Lowery's comments came in response to a report that "a prominent black leader worked with the FBI in its undercover campaign to replace King as head of the civil rights movement." On June 3, the *Atlanta Daily World* published an article identifying that black leader as Roy Wilkins, the former head of the National Association for the Advancement of Colored People (NAACP).

Lowery gave a "blistering" response to these new charges, declaring that "black folks in particular and the nation in general must see through this vicious effort to shift a portion of the blame for attacks on Dr. King to the black community.... The fact that Wilkins had conversation[s] with the FBI in no way indicates that he collaborated with them to discredit Dr. King and the movement.... We're all aware ... that in the mid-60's Mr. [J. Edgar] Hoover had a fierce determination to discredit

Dr. King and thereby weaken the civil rights movement by establishing the Communist influence or by any other means." (Also see entries dated November 19, 1975, and November 17, 1978.)

June 3. Several hundred people gathered at a hotel in Atlanta, Georgia, to pay tribute to Ruby Hurley on the occasion of her retirement from the NAACP after more than thirty years of service.

A native of Washington, D.C., Hurley joined the NAACP after heading a committee that had worked to establish singer Marian Anderson's right to perform at Constitution Hall in the capital in 1939. (See entry dated March, 1939). In 1943, she became the organization's national youth director. During her eight years in the position, the NAACP's membership tripled to 92 college chapters and 178 youth councils, enrolling 25,000 members.

Following her success in the Youth Division of the NAACP, Hurley headed south in 1951 to coordinate membership campaigns and revive inactive branches. Out of these activities grew the NAACP's Southeastern Regional Office, which included the states of Alabama, Florida, Georgia, Mississippi, North Carolina, South Carolina, and Tennessee. It became the largest region of the entire NAACP.

Hurley began her work in the South in 1951, the same year that a Christmas night bomb killed Harry T. Moore, the NAACP's Florida coordinator, and his wife, Harriett. Hate and violence became her constant companions for the next twenty-seven years. Hurley herself investigated many of the most terrible racial crimes of the 1950s and sent copies of her reports to both the NAACP and the FBI.

Hurley looked back on her life's work in an interview published in the *Atlanta Constitution* on May 30, 1978. In particular, she recalled her attempts to gather information about the 1955 lynching of black teenager Emmett Till in Mississippi. Witnesses who were afraid to talk to anyone else about the crime agreed to discuss it with Hurley after she disguised herself as a field hand and went from plantation to plantation to gather information. "I must have been crazy," she declared. "Young people talk about what they would have done if they were living during those times.... But they wouldn't have done anything. They couldn't have done any more than their elders."

Commenting on present and future trends, Hurley remarked: "I started worrying about black young people when I heard them saying they're black and they're proud. But just being black is no reason to be proud.... My feeling is that if you're going to be proud, you ought to have some knowledge (about the history of the black race) to build a basis to be proud. You won't have to go bragging that you're black and proud."

June 25. Abraham Lincoln Davis, a founder of the Southern Christian Leadership Conference (SCLC) and the first black city councilman in New Orleans, Louisiana, died there at the age of sixty-three.

The pastor of the New Zion Baptist Church in New Orleans for forty-three years, Davis met there with Martin Luther King, Jr., and other civil rights activists in 1957 to organize the SCLC. The group members chose King as their first president and Davis as vice-president. Davis was elected to the New Orleans City Council in January, 1975.

June 28. In a serious blow to affirmative action (the term used to describe efforts to improve opportunities for minorities and women), the U.S. Supreme Court ordered that white student Allan P. Bakke be admitted to the Medical College of the University of California at Davis.

The Court indicated that the school's refusal to admit Bakke was a case of reverse discrimination because qualified white applicants had been turned down in favor of minorities. While it agreed that the goal of creating a diverse student body was constitutional, the Court ruled that using racial or ethnic quotas was not the right way to achieve racial balance.

August 20. The *Detroit Free Press* published details of documents obtained by the American Civil Liberties Union (ACLU) that showed that in 1961, the FBI had passed along information about two Freedom Rider buses to a Birmingham, Alabama, police sergeant who was "a known Ku Klux Klan agent."

The documents were released to ACLU attorneys for seventy-eight-year-old Walter Bergman, a former professor at Wayne State University in Detroit. He had filed suit against the FBI claiming that he was partially paralyzed from a beating he suffered at the hands of Ku Klux Klansmen when they intercepted a Freedom Riders' bus in Anniston, Alabama (fifty miles east of Birmingham). On the same day, a similar Klan assault occurred in Birmingham.

Howard Simon, executive director of the Michigan ACLU, said that the documents showed that the FBI's "failure to provide protection provoked" the assaults on the Freedom Riders. (Also see entries dated May 4, 1961, and February 7, 1984.)

August 20. Lee Elder, one of the few professional black golfers in the United States, claimed first prize of $300,000 in the Westchester Golf Classic in Harrison, New York.

The forty-four-year-old Elder won with a score of 274, which is ten under par on the 6,603-yard Westchester Country Club course. He called the victory "a little more significant to me personally" than his historic feat three years earlier, when he became the first black to compete in the Masters Tournament in Augusta, Georgia. (See entry dated April 8, 1975.)

September 7. The Southern Christian Leadership Conference (SCLC) office in Jacksonville, Florida, reported that within the preceding week it had received twenty-two complaints from black soldiers of "abusive treatment" at Fort Stewart-Hunter near Savannah, Georgia. The head of the Jacksonville SCLC office said white officers and non-commissioned officers were harassing blacks with harsh treatment and inflammatory insults such as "nigger."

These incidents followed an announcement in August that the Army was planning to launch a year-long study to find out why black soldiers were being punished and dishonorably discharged at a rate about twice that of white soldiers. In addition, the study was going to look into why black soldiers were being charged with more serious offenses than white soldiers.

September 15. Muhammad Ali regained the World Boxing Association's (WBA) heavyweight championship in a unanimous decision over Leon Spinks in New Orleans, Louisiana. Ali thus became the first heavyweight boxer to win the championship three times.

October 7. Veteran Democratic Congressman Charles Diggs from Michigan was convicted in a federal district court in Washington, D.C., of using the mails to defraud and file false payroll vouchers. The latter charge stemmed from "a scheme to require his staff members to give him money from their padded pay raises so he could pay off huge personal debts."

A founder of the Congressional Black Caucus (CBC), Diggs had been overwhelmingly reelected by voters in his Detroit, Michigan, district just the week before his conviction.

November 17. Two agents of the Federal Bureau of Investigation (FBI) testified before the Select Committee on Assassinations of the U.S. House of Representatives that the Bureau's eleven-year surveillance of Dr. Martin Luther King, Jr., "was based solely" on the late FBI Director J. Edgar Hoover's "hatred of the civil rights leader." (See entries dated November 19, 1975, and May 29-June 3, 1978.) The two agents did not, however, link the FBI directly to the murder of King.

In 1975, however, another FBI agent who was testifying before the U.S. Senate's Select Committee on Intelligence raised some doubts about that same issue. "It just defies reason to say that the same people who have engaged in a 10-year vendetta against Dr. King should investigate his murder," he observed.

In a syndicated column published in the *Atlanta Constitution* on September 11, 1978, civil rights leader Jesse Jackson said "circumstantial evidence" suggested that the FBI was "deeply implicated" in King's assassination. Jackson was one of the people with King when the fatal bullet struck him on April 4, 1968.

1979   **August 15.** Andrew Young resigned from his post as the U.S. Ambassador to the United Nations, explaining that he "could not promise to muzzle himself and stay out of controversies that might prove politically embarrassing to President [Jimmy] Carter." The African American diplomat said that he didn't "feel a bit sorry for a thing I have done. I have tried to interpret to our country some of the mood of the rest of the world. Unfortunately, but by birth, I come from the ranks of those who had known and identified with some level of oppression in the world.... I could not say that given the same situation, I wouldn't do it again, almost exactly the same way."

Young's brief career as the first black UN ambassador from the United States had been very controversial. He had made American relations with African nations a top priority while at the same time condemning such leading western democracies as Great Britain and Sweden as racist.

His downfall came after he held an unauthorized meeting in July, 1979, with a representative of the Palestine Liberation Organization (PLO). The U.S. government considered the PLO a terrorist organization and strongly disapproved of such contacts with the group. Young was also accused of not telling the State Department about the talks and of giving "only a partial and inaccurate version of events when he was asked."

When news of the meeting between Young and the PLO became public, many influential Americans called for his removal from office. Yet African American civil rights leader Jesse Jackson defended the former ambassador and accused President Carter of sacrificing "Africa, the third world, and black Americans." (Also see entries dated January 30, 1977, and October 3, 1977.)

1980

January 25. The nation's first and only African American-owned cable network, Black Entertainment Television (BET), marked its first day on the air. Its founder and chairman was Robert L. Johnson.

At first, programs were broadcast only on Fridays from 11 p.m. until 2 a.m. As of 1992, BET had become a twenty-four-hour, seven-day-a-week operation that reached more than thirty-three million households. It also owns *YSB* (*Young Sisters and Brothers*), a magazine for black teens, and *Emerge,* a news-oriented magazine for African American professionals.

March 31. Jesse Owens, hero of the 1936 Olympics, died in Phoenix, Arizona. (Also see entry dated August 9, 1936.)

May 18. At least fifteen people died after two nights of racial rioting in the Liberty City neighborhood of Miami, Florida. The violence was sparked by a controversial verdict in a case of alleged police brutality. The disturbances were the worst in the nation since the black ghettos of Watts and Detroit erupted in the late 1960s.

The riot began on May 17 after news came from Tampa, Florida, that an all-male, all-white jury had found four white deputy sheriffs from Dade County (of which Miami is the county seat) not guilty of killing a black insurance executive named Arthur McDuffie. The deputies had been charged with beating McDuffie to death and then making it look as if he had died in a motorcycle accident. The trial had been held in Tampa because a Dade County judge had ruled that the case was "a racial time bomb" in Miami.

During the riot, snipers shot at cars, civilians, and police. Three Miami police officers were wounded by gunfire on May 18. At least two of the rioters were shot dead by police. Florida governor Bob Graham called up 1,100 National Guardsmen, 300 highway patrol officers, four helicopters, and an armored personnel carrier to assist local law enforcement authorities. At least 216 people were injured as a result of the violence, and widespread looting and property damage were reported.

As the riot progressed, a grassroots black organization presented Miami mayor Maurice Feree with a set of eleven demands. Feree said he thought the city could meet at least nine of the demands, including some related to the hiring and promotion of blacks. He also said he would consider granting amnesty to all of those accused of looting. But Feree could not agree with the demand to fire State Attorney Janet Reno, the prosecutor in the McDuffie case.

After the riot, U.S. Attorney Atlee Wampler III said that evidence already assembled by the FBI in the McDuffie case would be presented to a federal grand jury in Miami on May 20, 1980.

May 29. The National Urban League (NUL)'s executive director, Vernon Jordan, was the target of an assassination attempt as he returned to his motel after giving a speech in Fort Wayne, Indiana.

Critically wounded with a gunshot to the back, Jordan spent the next few months in the hospital and was not able to go back to work until that fall. (Police never found the would-be killer.) About a year later, he quit the NUL to practice law. (Also see entries dated June 15, 1971, and November 3, 1992.)

November. Republican Ronald Reagan defeated Democrat Jimmy Carter in a landslide to become the fortieth president of the United States.

December 22. President-elect Ronald Reagan named black lawyer Samuel Pierce, Jr., to the post of Secretary of Housing and Urban Development (HUD). At the time of his appointment, he was serving as a partner in a prestigious New York law firm. Pierce was the only minority person selected to join the new president's cabinet. (Also see entry dated September 20, 1989.)

1981   **April 12.** Boxer Joe Louis, the famous "Brown Bomber," died at the age of sixty-seven. (Also see entries dated June 25, 1935; June 22, 1938; and June 22, 1993.)

September 8. Roy Wilkins, head of the National Association for the Advancement of Colored People (NAACP) from 1955 until 1977, died in New York City at the age of eighty.

Wilkins had quietly but effectively led the NAACP through some of the most important battles of the civil rights movement, especially those that were fought in the courtroom. Because he and the NAACP rejected the extremism of black power supporters during the 1960s, they lost their appeal among many younger and more radical blacks. But by the time of Wilkins's death, he was acknowledged as one of the "giants" along with leaders such as Martin Luther King, Jr. (Also see entry dated April 11, 1955.)

November 16. President Ronald Reagan fired Arthur S. Flemming, the chairman of the U.S. Commission on Civil Rights (CCR). Sources told United Press International (UPI) that the administration was angry with Flemming's strong support for affirmative action, voting rights, and busing to achieve school integration.

President Reagan then appointed Clarence Pendleton, Jr., a fifty-year-old black Californian, to replace Flemming and thus become the CCR's first black chairman. Considered a conservative Republican, Pendleton had supported Reagan in the 1980 elections. He had previously served as chairman of the San Diego Transit Corporation and head of the San Diego Urban League.

1982

February 10. Noting her husband's health problems and the growing conservatism in Washington, longtime Representative Shirley Chisholm announced her retirement from Congress. (See entries dated November 5, 1968; January 25, 1972; and July 12, 1972.)

Since then, she has remained very active in teaching, lecturing, and Democratic politics, especially as a founder and first leader of the National Political Congress of Black Women.

February 17. Jazz pianist Thelonious Monk died after suffering a massive stroke. He had played a vital role in the jazz revolution of the early 1940s as both a musician and a composer and was a pioneer in the development of bop (a type of jazz).

Born October 10, 1917, in Rocky Mount, North Carolina, Monk moved with his family to New York City in the early 1920s. When he was eleven, he began supplementing his gospel training with weekly piano lessons and soon was accompanying the Baptist choir in which his mother sang.

Just two years later, Monk was playing in a trio at a local bar and grill. He eventually won so many of the weekly Apollo Theater amateur contests that he was banned from entering any more. At the age of sixteen, he left school to travel with an evangelical faith healer and preacher. When he returned home the following year, he formed his first group. With the exception of some brief work with the Lucky Millander band and Coleman Hawkins, Monk generally led his own small groups throughout his career.

During the early 1940s, Monk found himself in the midst of a new wave of jazz music. Bebop, a faster and more complex style than the older "swing" style of jazz, grew out of late-night jam sessions at jazz clubs. (Perhaps the most famous of these was Minton's, where Monk was the house pianist.) In fact, *Keyboard* magazine claimed "Monk was at the eye of what would become the bebop hurricane." His own music, however, was developing a unique style, and by the early 1950s he had composed the classics "Blue Monk," "Round Midnight," and "Epistrophy."

At first, only a small circle of fans appreciated his angular melodies, harmonies marked by jarring surprises, and unusual treatment of notes (and even the absence of notes). But over the years Monk came to be recognized as one of the founding fathers of modern jazz. Some people now consider him to be the most important jazz composer since Duke Ellington.

In 1951, Monk's career (which was already faltering) was dealt a serious blow when he was charged with possession of narcotics. He ended up in jail for two months and, more importantly, New York state officials took away his cabaret card. Without it, he could not play any local club dates.

Within a few years, however, his luck changed and his career revived. Monk gave a series of concerts in Paris in 1954, he cut his first solo album, *Pure Monk,* and signed with the Riverside label. In 1957, he had an eight-month engagement at New York's Five Spot, where devoted fans of his music gathered to hear their idol play. It was there that he also met jazz newcomer John Coltrane.

Over the next few years, Monk made several recordings for Riverside, including *Brilliant Corners, Thelonious Himself,* and *Monk with Coltrane.* These recordings were so successful that in 1962 Columbia offered Monk a well-paying contract. In 1964 *Time* magazine featured his picture on the cover, a rare honor for a jazz musician.

Living up to the *New York Post*'s description of him as "one of jazz's great eccentrics," Monk began to withdraw from the public eye beginning in the mid-1960s. From then until his death, he made only a few solo and trio recordings for Black Lion in London and gave an occasional concert.

Monk's son, T. S. Monk, Jr., is also a musician whose specialty is the drums. His recording, *Take One,* is a tribute to his father and other bop composers.

February 27. Wayne Williams, a self-described entertainment "talent scout," was convicted of murder in the slayings of Jimmy Ray Payne, age twenty-one, and Nathaniel Cater, age twenty-seven, in Atlanta, Georgia. The conviction came after one of the largest manhunts in U.S. history. The search—which attracted national attention—eventually pointed to the twenty-three-year-old Williams as America's first black serial killer.

Payne and Cater were two of the twenty-eight young blacks, mostly males under the age of twenty-one, who were killed in Atlanta during a twenty-two-month period beginning in 1979. Most of the victims were strangled. Together, the slayings became known as "the Atlanta Child Murder Cases."

Psychics, writers, civil rights activists, and others offered theories on the motives and identities of the killer or killers. Many believed that Ku Klux Klansmen or other white supremacists were responsible. And, since most of the victims were young black males, some people thought that a homosexual had committed the crimes.

On May 22, 1981, law enforcement officers on stakeout along the Chattahoochee River in north Atlanta heard a loud splash. A short time later, other officers questioned and held Wayne Williams after they noticed him driving slowly with his headlights dimmed across a Chattahoochee River bridge. Two days later, the body of twenty-seven-year-old Nathaniel Cater was found floating in the river. On June 21, 1981, Williams was arrested and charged with the murders of Cater and Jimmy Ray Payne.

Williams, who took the stand in his own defense during the trial, strongly denied that he had committed the murders. However, the prosecution found witnesses who said they had seen him with seven of the victims. Other evidence against Williams included fibers taken from clothing and other fabrics and bloodstains found in his car. On February 27, 1982, after deliberating for eleven hours, a majority black jury found Williams guilty of two counts of murder. The presiding judge, Clarence Cooper, also an African American, sentenced Williams to two consecutive life terms in prison. The defense promised an immediate appeal.

May 6. Loretta Glickman, a thirty-six-year-old African American investment counselor, was elected mayor of Pasadena, California, by the city's Board of Directors. This made Glickman the first black woman to become mayor of a major city in the United States.

August 21. Calvin Simmons, regarded as one of the country's most promising young black orchestra conductors, drowned after his boat capsized in a pond in Lake Placid, New York. The thirty-two-year-old African American had led the Oakland (California) Symphony Orchestra.

December 4. Herschel Walker, African American running back for the University of Georgia, won the Heisman Trophy, football's highest collegiate award. A native of Wrightsville, Georgia, Walker was the seventh person to capture the Heisman in his junior year. The nation's football writers had previously named him to the All-America team three times.

December 28-29. A new wave of racial violence erupted in Miami, Florida, after a Hispanic police officer, Luis Alvarez, shot and killed twenty-one-year-old Nevell Johnson, Jr., a suspected black looter.

The disturbance in the Overtown section of the city left two people dead and twenty-seven wounded. Dozens of businesses were destroyed or damaged, and forty-three people were arrested. Although up to 200 people were involved in the rioting, it was not as serious as the racial violence in Miami's Liberty City area in 1980. (See entry dated May 18, 1980.)

1983

February 12. Eubie Blake, African American ragtime pianist and composer, died in Brooklyn, New York, just five days after celebrating his 100th birthday. (Also see entry dated 1921.)

February 16. Luis Alvarez, a police officer in Miami, Florida, was indicted by a Dade County Grand Jury for manslaughter in the shooting death of Nevell Johnson, Jr., a twenty-one-year-old black man. The incident had sparked two days of racial rioting in the Overtown section of Miami. (See entry dated December 28, 1982.)

February 23. Former African American congressman Harold Washington defeated Mayor Jane Byrne to win the Democratic primary election for mayor of Chicago, Illinois.

His victory came after a bitter and racially divisive campaign. Although the sixty-year-old Washington appealed to whites for their votes, he built the foundation of his quest on turning out a solid bloc of black voters. He repeatedly told them that "it's our turn.... We don't need to apologize for it, and we're not going to waste a lot of time explaining it.... It's our turn—that's all." (Also see entry dated April 12, 1983.)

February 23. Herschel Walker, the African American collegiate football player who had received the Heisman Trophy in December, 1982, signed "the biggest contract in football history" with the New Jersey Generals of the United States Football League. The value of the three-year contract was estimated at more than $8 million. Walker passed up his senior year at the University of Georgia in order to join the Generals.

April 12. Former Democratic congressman Harold Washington defeated Republican lawyer Bernard Epton to become the first black mayor of Chicago, Illinois. His victory was made possible by a very heavy turnout of black voters, strong Hispanic support, and some support from middle-class whites, although the election had been marked by serious racial divisions. (Also see entry dated February 23, 1983.)

April 19-20. On April 19, about 100 black students prayed and sang in front of the administration building at the University of Mississippi in Oxford to protest the use of the Confederate flag as a symbol of the university. During the previous night, several hundred white students had waved the flag and sung the Confederate battle song, "Dixie," in front of a black fraternity house on the campus. A black student told reporters that the whites also yelled "nigger night" and "save the flag."

During the fall of 1982, some black students at the university had called for a ban on the rebel flag, the display of the Colonel Reb cartoon mascot, and the singing of "Dixie" at athletic events. They said the Confederate symbols were both "racist and offensive."

On April 20, the university's chancellor announced that the Confederate flag would no longer be used as a school symbol. But black students complained because he did not stop people from continuing to wave the flag on campus or at athletic events. He also did not ban the use of the Colonel Reb mascot or the singing of "Dixie." A group of white students cheered the chancellor's announcement and waved Confederate flags.

May 12. Lou Gossett, Jr. won an Academy Award as Best Supporting Actor for his role as a Marine Corps drill sergeant in the film *An Officer and a Gentleman.* He became only the third black actor or actress to win an Oscar in the fifty-five-year history of the awards. (See entries dated March, 1940, and April 13, 1964.)

Gossett, age forty-four, had won an Emmy Award in 1977 for his role as "Fiddler" in the ABC miniseries "Roots." (See entry dated September 11, 1977.) As he received his Oscar, blacks demonstrated outside the Hollywood Music Center calling the Academy Awards "a racist affair." In reaction to the protest, Gossett commented: "You shouldn't call anything racist if [it is] improving." He expressed the hope that his award would "catch on like measles" and lead to the creation of more roles for black actors and actresses in Hollywood.

June 17. Nelson W. Trout, a professor and director of minority studies at Trinity Lutheran Seminary in Columbus, Ohio, was elected Bishop of the American Lutheran Church's South Pacific District in California. This made him the first black person ever elected to full-time office in the American Lutheran Church, traditionally the church of Scandinavian and Germanic ethnic groups in the East and Midwest.

June 22. The State Senate of Louisiana repealed the last of the nation's racial classification laws. The unanimous senate action followed a 90-4 vote for repeal in the Louisiana House of Representatives on June 9, 1983. The racial classification law had defined a black person as anyone "with one-thirty secondth 'Negro' blood."

September 17. Vanessa Williams, a twenty-year-old African American junior at New York's Syracuse University, was crowned "Miss America" for 1984. It was the first time in the history of the sixty-year-old pageant that a black woman had won the title. In fact, for half of the pageant's history, black females had not even been allowed to enter the competition.

November 2. President Ronald Reagan signed a bill establishing a federal holiday in honor of slain civil rights leader Martin Luther King, Jr. The holiday was scheduled to begin in 1986 on the third Monday in January.

Many Americans, including singer Stevie Wonder (who composed and recorded a birthday song honoring King) and Coretta Scott King, the civil rights leader's widow, had lobbied for the holiday ever since King's assassination in 1968. (Also see entry dated January 20, 1986.)

November 11. Representatives from the U.S. Congress and the Reagan administration reached an agreement to continue funding the U.S. Commission on Civil Rights (CCR). Established in 1957, the CCR is an advisory group that investigates reports of discrimination and recommends steps for Congress and the president to take to correct it.

Earlier, President Reagan had tried to replace but eventually fired three Democratic members of the Commission who disagreed with him on busing to achieve school desegregation and affirmative action in job-discrimination cases. (See entry dated November 16, 1981.) Many congressmen complained that Reagan was trying to destroy "the commission's independence and integrity," so on September 30, 1983, they refused to approve the funds needed to keep running the CCR.

Under the new agreement between Congress and the Reagan administration, the commission would have eight members instead of six. The president and Congress would each name four members to serve staggered six-year terms, and members could not be fired just for political reasons. Also, Congress would be allowed to reappoint two of the three commissioners President Reagan had let go—Democrats Mary Frances Berry (an African American) and Blandina C. Ramirez (a Hispanic).

1984

January 2. W. Wilson Goode, the forty-five-year-old son of North Carolina sharecroppers, was inaugurated as mayor of Philadelphia, Pennsylvania. Goode became the first African American chief executive in the city's 301-year history. At the time of his inauguration, about 40 percent of Philadelphia's 1.6 million people were black.

January 6. Robert N.C. Nix, Jr., was inaugurated as chief justice of the Pennsylvania Supreme Court. This made him the first African American to sit on a state Supreme Court bench since the Reconstruction era.

Michael Jackson

January 16. The American Music Awards presented the Award of Merit to African American pop singer Michael Jackson at its eleventh annual ceremonies. The award recognized Jackson's "outstanding contributions over a long period of time to the musical entertainment of the American public." Previous African American winners of the award included Berry Gordy, Jr., founder of Motown Records, and singers Ella Fitzgerald and Stevie Wonder.

January 22. Marcus Allen, African American running back for the Los Angeles Raiders, was named Most Valuable Player (MVP) of Super Bowl XXVIII in Tampa, Florida. Allen gained a record 191 yards rushing on twenty carries and scored two touchdowns, one on a five-yard run, the other on a 74-yard run. The Raiders defeated the Washington Redskins by a score of 38-9.

February 2. Mobile County Circuit Court Judge Braxton Kittrell sentenced Ku Klux Klansman Henry Hays to death for the 1981 murder of Michael Donald. Donald was a nineteen-year-old black youth who was beaten, slashed across the throat, and then hung from a tree in downtown Mobile, Alabama. Hays, age twenty-nine, had been convicted of murder by a jury of eleven whites and one black on December 10, 1983. The jury had recommended a sentence of life in prison.

February 7. A U.S. District Court judge in Kalamazoo, Michigan, awarded a judgment of $50,000 to Walter Bergman, an eighty-four-year-old former Freedom Rider.

Ku Klux Klansmen had beaten Bergman at an Alabama bus station in 1961. The assault left him partially paralyzed. He argued in court that the FBI knew the Klan planned to attack the Freedom Riders and did nothing to stop it. The judge agreed that there was plenty of evidence to support his claim. (Also see entries dated May 4, 1961, and August 20, 1978.)

February 28. The U.S. Supreme Court ruled that federal laws banning racial or sexual discrimination by schools and colleges apply only to the affected program or activity, not to the entire institution.

The administration of President Ronald Reagan applauded the decision. But many congressmen, women's rights supporters, and civil rights groups reacted with alarm. They were afraid that even though the Court's ruling had to do with sex discrimination, it could also be applied to civil rights cases.

In fact, in the months following the decision, federal agencies did indeed drop or limit hundreds of civil rights cases. (Also see entries dated March 16, 1988; March 20, 1988; and March 22, 1988.)

March 28. Benjamin Mays, educator and civil rights spokesperson, died of heart failure in Atlanta, Georgia, at the age of eighty-nine.

Mays was born August 1, 1894, in Epworth, South Carolina. His parents were former slaves and tenant farmers. In 1928, Mays graduated with honors from Bates College in Lewiston, Maine. While attending graduate school at the University of Chicago, he held a variety of teaching jobs and also served as a Baptist minister. He received his doctorate degree from the University of Chicago in 1935.

Mays was dean of the School of Religion at Howard University from 1934 until 1940, at which time he became president of Morehouse College in Atlanta. The highly respected school was then facing some serious problems that threatened its future. The Depression had left it in financial trouble, and student enrollment had dropped after many young men decided to look for work in the booming wartime economy instead.

But through his skills as a speechmaker and a fundraiser, Mays was eventually able to restore Morehouse's vitality and prestige. He expanded the programs that former president John Hope had begun, which enabled the college to produce an outstanding group of black business and professional men as well as civil rights leaders such as Martin Luther King, Jr.

Also like John Hope, Mays became known as a militant civil rights advocate. As he explained years later: "I was born a little stubborn on the race issue.... I felt that no man had a right to look down on another man. Every man, whether he's on the right of you, the left of you, certainly in back of you—it makes no difference—is still a man." At the historic March on Washington in 1963, Mays led the opening prayer and gave a speech. Five years later, in an emotional eulogy at the funeral of Martin Luther King, Jr., he praised the slain civil rights leader and blamed his death on America's racist society.

Mays served on the NAACP board of directors and wrote hundreds of essays in magazines, newspapers, and scholarly journals condemning segregation and discrimination and pleading for racial justice and harmony. He wrote several books on the subject, too, including *A Gospel for Social Awakening* (1950), *Seeking to Be a Christian in Race Relations* (1957), *Disturbed about Man* (1969), and his autobiography, *Born to Rebel* (1971).

In 1969, two years after his retirement from Morehouse, Mays won a seat on the Atlanta Board of Education. The next year he was elected the group's first black president. He was reelected to the position six times over the next twelve years.

In commenting on Mays's death, Charlie Moreland, president of the Morehouse College Alumni Association, remembered one of Mays's favorite quotations: "It must be born in mind that not reaching your goal is not tragic. The tragedy lies in not having a goal to reach."

April 1. In Los Angeles, California, Motown singer, songwriter, and musician Marvin Gaye was shot to death by his father during an argument between the two men.

Born in 1939 in Washington, D.C., Gaye entered the music business in 1957 as a member of the Marquees, a Washington-based rhythm and blues vocal group. At a concert in Detroit, Michigan, in 1961, Gaye met up-and-coming music producer Berry Gordy and signed on with Motown Records as a solo artist.

At first, Gaye did background instrumentals for various Motown performers, including Smokey Robinson. But soon he was one of the company's hottest vocalists. His pop-soul hits from the 1960s—including "Can I Get a Witness," "How Sweet It Is to Be Loved by You," and "I Heard It through the Grapevine"— are considered classics. He and Tammi Terrell also topped the charts during those years with a number of romantic ballads such as "You're All I Need to Get By" and "Ain't Nothin' Like the Real Thing."

Terrell's death from a brain tumor in 1970 had a profound effect on Gaye, who left the music business briefly. He returned in 1971 with an album entitled *What's Going On* that was very different from his previous Motown recordings. The songs Gaye wrote, sang, and played for this ground-breaking album dealt with social issues such as pollution, the Vietnam War, drug addiction, and ghetto life. The title song and two others, "Mercy, Mercy Me" and "Inner City Blues," all made it into the top ten on the pop charts.

Gaye followed this up with more romantic music, this time more seductively sexual than the glossy soul hits Motown was famous for during the 1960s. But by the mid-1970s he had become heavily involved with cocaine, and his career went downhill.

In 1982, Gaye began a promising comeback with an album called *Midnight Love* that featured the hit song, "Sexual Healing." It won two Grammy Awards in 1983 and prompted the singer to go on his first concert tour in seven years. He still had not been able to overcome his cocaine habit, however. It contributed to the problems between father and son that left Gaye dead just one day before his forty-fifth birthday.

April 26. William "Count" Basie, African American bandleader, died of cancer in Hollywood, Florida, at the age of seventy-nine.

Born in 1904, Basie grew up in Red Bank, New Jersey, and began taking music lessons at the age of eight. Despite his protests, his mother insisted that he was "going to learn how to play the piano if it kills you."

Basie began playing professionally during the early 1920s on the vaudeville circuit. In the late 1920s, he joined Walter Page's Blue Devils group in Kansas City, Missouri. After that band broke up in 1929, Basie joined Benny Moten's band. When Moten died a few years later, Basie took over and began his own group, the ten-piece Count Basie Band.

The group was not really "discovered" until 1935 when John Hammond, a jazz promoter who had helped make singer Billie Holiday famous, saw them perform in Kansas City. He was so impressed that he urged Basie to increase the size of his band and then booked them on their first national tour.

It was while he was still in Kansas City that Basie acquired his famous nickname, "Count." A radio announcer was discussing the "royal family" of jazz—including the "Duke of Ellington" and the "King of Oliver"—and hit upon the idea of a "Count of Basie." Basie never really liked the nickname, however. As he explained in 1982, "I wanted to be called Buck or Hoot or even Arkansas Fats," all of whom were silent-film heroes.

By 1936, only a year after their "discovery," Basie and his band had earned a reputation that reached far beyond Kansas City. They travelled widely throughout the country and made their home base at the Roseland Ballroom in New York City.

Basie's trademark was his clean, light keyboard touch and laid-back conducting style. In his book *Night Creature* (1980), jazz critic Whitney Balliett noted: "[Basie] pilots his ship from the keyboard with an occasional raised finger, an almost imperceptible nod, a sudden widely opened eye, a left-hand chord, a lifted chin, a smile, and plays background and solo piano that is the quintessence of swinging and taste and good cheer, even when almost nothing happens around it."

The Basie band began recording in 1937. Their early albums included *Basie's Back in Town, Blues by Basie,* and *Super Chief.* Basie tunes such as the jazz classic "One O'Clock Jump" demonstrated the band's mastery of what one writer terms "call-and-response phrasing." With this technique, for example, the saxophones would play a simple blues refrain and the brass section would "answer" them with their own improvised creation.

During the early 1950s, Basie began to cut down the size of his band. He then collaborated with blues singer "Big" Joe Williams in what many people believed was a creative peak for both performers. Basie's popularity lasted throughout the rest of the 1950s and on into the 1960s, 1970s, and even the 1980s. He and his band made many successful world tours and continued to record.

Basie's last performance was at the Hollywood Palladium on March 19, 1984, just five weeks before his death. It marked the end of a career that spanned more than fifty years. (Also see entry dated February 26, 1985.)

June 12. The U.S. Supreme Court ruled that employers may not eliminate seniority plans that favor white men in order to protect "affirmative action gains by minorities and women when hard times hit." The Court also ruled that special preferences to correct past discrimination were available only to people who could prove they had been victimized by such bias, not to "a class of people such as all blacks in an employer's work force."

Civil rights advocates regarded this decision as a major defeat. (Also see entries dated June 25, 1976; June 28, 1978; January 23, 1989; and June 12, 1989.)

August 4-11. At the Summer Olympic Games held in Los Angeles, California, several African American athletes captured the coveted gold medal for their first-place finishes in various events.

On August 4, Carl Lewis won the finals of the prestigious 100-meter dash, earning the United States its first gold medal in track and field in the 1984 games. He ran it in 9.99 seconds, the fastest 100 meters ever run at sea level in Olympic history.

On August 5, Evelyn Ashford set an Olympic record of 10.97 seconds while winning the women's 100-meter finals, and Edwin Moses won the 400-meter intermediate hurdles in 49.75 seconds.

On August 11, Carl Lewis completed his sweep of four gold medals by running the last leg of the U.S. 400-meter relay team. He went 100 meters in 8.94 seconds, enabling the Americans to set the first track and field record of the 1984 Games, 37.83 seconds. Earlier, Lewis had won gold medals in the 100-meter dash (see above), the 200-meter dash, and the long jump.

Lewis's feats in the 1984 Olympics equalled those of Jesse Owens, the African American who won four gold medals in the same events in the 1936 Olympics in Berlin, Germany. (See entry dated August 9, 1936.) Commenting on his achievements, Lewis told reporters, "It is an honor. Two years ago, everyone in the world said it couldn't be done. Even a year ago, I said I couldn't do it." He added, "I was looking for Ruth Owens [Jesse Owens's widow]. Jesse has been such an inspiration to me. I wanted to dedicate one medal to her."

November 6. Ronald Reagan was reelected president of the United States by the biggest margin in recent history over his Democratic opponent, former vice-president Walter Mondale. By most estimates, Reagan received only 20 percent of the African American vote. Civil rights leaders had frequently criticized him during his first term for being insensitive to black issues.

November 11. Martin Luther King, Sr., minister, civil rights activist, and father of slain civil rights leader, Martin Luther King, Jr., died following a heart attack in Atlanta, Georgia. He was eighty-four.

King was born Michael Luther King to a sharecropper and cleaning woman in Stockbridge, Georgia, on December 19, 1899. (He changed his name in 1934 to honor the famous German religious scholar Martin Luther.) At age seventeen, he moved to Atlanta and became a minister. He also attended Morehouse College, graduating in 1930. A year later King succeeded his father-in-law, Adam Daniel Williams, as pastor of the Ebenezer Baptist Church, one of Atlanta's largest black congregations. He remained as pastor or co-pastor of the church until 1975.

Even before King became pastor of Ebenezer Baptist Church, he had become active in civic, political, and racial affairs in Atlanta. In 1924, for example, he was one of the black leaders who successfully lobbied for the construction of the Booker T. Washington High School, the first secondary school for blacks in the city. In 1936, King was a leader in a voting rights march to Atlanta's City Hall. And in 1961, he participated in protests against segregated cafeterias in the city and helped negotiate an agreement for their desegregation.

King was also a director of Citizens Trust Company, the city's black bank. He served as a member of the board of directors or trustees of SCLC, Morehouse College, the Morehouse School of Religion, and the Carrie Steele-Pitts Orphans Home. In 1972, the Atlanta chapter of the National Conference of Christians and Jews named him "Clergyman of the Year."

Although King lost his famous son to an assassin's bullet in 1968 and his wife to another assassin in 1974, he continued to insist, "I don't hate.... There is no time for that, and no reason either. Nothing that a man does takes him lower than when he allows himself to fall so low as to hate anyone."

December 31. The United Negro College Fund (UNCF), a fund-raising organization for most of the nation's private black colleges and universities, announced that it had raised more than $14.1 million in pledges during a national telethon. Hosted by singer Lou Rawls, the event was the first of its kind carried on national television. Organizers had set a goal of $15 million in pledges.

1985

January 7. Lou Brock, African American outfielder for the St. Louis Cardinals of the National Baseball League, was elected to the Baseball Hall of Fame at Cooperstown, New York.

Brock played in the major leagues from 1961 until 1975. He began his career with the Chicago Cubs, but spent most of it with the St. Louis Cardinals. At the time of his election to the Hall of Fame, Brock still led all players in the number of bases stolen with 938, held the National League record of 118 bases stolen in one season (1974), and held the highest batting average for World Series games (.391) in 21 games.

February 26. Several African American entertainers received awards during the presentations of the 1984 Grammys, the highest honors for recording artists.

Tina Turner, the "Queen of Rhythm and Blues," won three Grammys, including Record of the Year and Song of the Year for "What's Love Got to Do with It?" Three Grammys also went to Prince for Best Rock Performance by a Group and Best Original Film Score for *Purple Rain*. For his songwriting efforts, Prince won Best New Rhythm and Blues Song for "I Feel for You." Lionel Richie's *Can't Slow Down* was named Album of the Year, and Chaka Khan was awarded a Grammy for her recording of "I Feel for You." Jazz trumpeter Wynton Marsalis won a Grammy in both the Jazz and Classical categories, the Pointer Sisters won two Grammys in the Pop category, and Shirley Caesar won two Grammys in the Gospel category. Michael Jackson won an award for his video *Making Michael Jackson's "Thriller."* Finally, the late Count Basie was awarded a Grammy for his orchestra's *88 Basie Street*.

May 5. The historic Apollo Theater in the Harlem section of New York City reopened to celebrate its 50th anniversary. The theater, which was once the top showplace for America's black entertainers, had been closed for fifteen months and had undergone more than $10 million in renovations. More than 1,500 people attended the reopening celebrations while another 2,000 stood outside.

The Apollo opened on 125th Street in Harlem in 1916 as an unnamed storefront and began featuring famous performers in 1935. Its earliest stars included comedians Jackie "Moms" Mabley and "Pigmeat" Markham. At the reopening ceremonies, many of the biggest names in black entertainment returned for an appearance, including comedian Bill Cosby and singers and dancers Patti LaBelle, Gregory Hines, Wilson Pickett, Little Richard, Stevie Wonder, and the Four Tops.

November 19. Veteran African American actor Lincoln Theodore Andrew Perry, better known as Stepin Fetchit, died of pneumonia and congestive heart failure in Woodland Hills, California. He was eighty-three years old.

A native of Key West, Florida, Perry took his stage name from a race horse on which he had won some money in Oklahoma before leaving for Hollywood in the 1920s. He began his acting career in the 1930s and appeared in such films as *Steamboat Round the Bend*. Perry was the first black performer to appear on film with such movie stars as Will Rogers and Shirley Temple.

His best-known film roles were usually "shuffling, head-scratching" servants, and many blacks viewed them as negative stereotypes of their race. Perry himself often grew angry at such criticism and defended his contributions to the acting profession. He once said that "when I came into motion pictures, it was as an individual.... I had no manager, and no one had the idea of making a Negro a star.... I became the first Negro entertainer to become a millionaire.... All the things that Bill Cosby and Sidney Poitier have done wouldn't be possible if I hadn't broken that law [the race barrier]. I set up thrones for them to come and sit on."

After the CBS television documentary entitled "Of Black America" characterized him as a "stupid, lazy, eye-rolling stereotype" in the 1960s, Perry sued the network, claiming that he had been held "up to hatred, contempt, [and] ridicule." A federal judge dismissed the suit in 1974.

1986   **January 16.** A bronze bust of Dr. Martin Luther King, Jr., was placed in the U.S. Capitol building. The statue was the first of any black American to stand in the halls of Congress. Created by John Wilson, a black artist at Boston University, the bust shows the civil rights leader in a thoughtful mood with a slightly bowed head. It was unveiled at the ceremonies by King's widow, Coretta Scott King.

January 18. A group of whites marched in downtown Raleigh, North Carolina, to honor the birthday of Confederate General Robert E. Lee and to protest the first federal holiday honoring Dr. Martin Luther King, Jr. Glenn Miller, leader of the White Patriots Party and a former Ku Klux Klansman, said that he was "nauseated and sickened" by the national tribute to King. Miller added, "We're down here to tell the world that we will never accept a birthday honoring a black communist. Never!"

The Raleigh demonstration was one of several protests and acts of vandalism directed at the first annual King holiday. In Buffalo, New York, for example, someone painted a bust of King displayed in a city park white. Elsewhere, several cities and states simply refused to recognize the holiday.

January 20. The nation celebrated the first national holiday in honor of slain civil rights leader Dr. Martin Luther King, Jr. It was the first such honor ever extended to an African American in U.S. history. (See entry dated November 2, 1983.)

In King's birthplace of Atlanta, Georgia, Vice-President George Bush and other political figures attended a wreath-laying ceremony at King's grave and an ecumenical service at Ebenezer Baptist Church, where King was the pastor at the time of his death. Also in the audience was Rosa Parks, whose refusal to give up her bus seat to a white man sparked the famous Montgomery, Alabama, bus boycott in 1955. In addition, the celebration included the first national Martin Luther King, Jr., Holiday Parade held in Atlanta.

January 28. Ronald McNair, an African American astronaut, died along with his six crew mates aboard the *Challenger* space shuttle when it exploded shortly after lift-off from Cape Canaveral, Florida. McNair, a thirty-five-year-old physicist, was the nation's second black astronaut.

September 30. Edward Perkins, a veteran diplomat, was named U.S. Ambassador to the Republic of South Africa. He was the first African American ever to serve in that position.

October 18. The NAACP, one of the nation's oldest and most prominent civil rights organizations, dedicated its new national headquarters in Baltimore, Maryland.

Founded in New York City in 1909, the NAACP left there partially because it could no longer afford the high rent and taxes. NAACP leaders chose Baltimore for the group's new headquarters largely because of "its majority black population and long history in promoting civil rights."

October 23. Five white students dressed in Ku Klux Klan-type attire broke into the room of Kevin Nesmith, a black cadet at The Citadel, a military college in South Carolina. The five students taunted Nesmith and left a charred paper cross in his room. Nesmith said that he slept through most of the incident. (Also see entry dated November 14-17, 1986.)

November 14-17. A black cadet at The Citadel who had been harassed by five white students resigned from the school, and a South Carolina State Commission issued a report on the original incident. (See entry dated October 23, 1986.)

On November 14, Kevin Nesmith resigned from the South Carolina military college because he felt he had been made to look like he was the "villain" in the hazing incident. But, he added, "the villains remain at Citadel." Nesmith also said

245

that "anger and frustration built up, and I felt mentally drained and no longer wanted to subject myself to this humiliation."

The five white cadets who cursed Nesmith in the October incident were suspended from the college, but the suspensions were delayed "on the condition they not get into any more serious trouble during the school year." They were also restricted to campus for the rest of the school year and "given additional marching tours."

But some black leaders in the state insisted that the school should have expelled the five cadets. The NAACP filed a lawsuit against The Citadel, claiming that Nesmith's civil rights had been violated and that the school historically had "tolerated and sanctioned" racial bigotry. On November 17, civil rights leader Jesse Jackson met with Nesmith and later requested a congressional investigation of race relations at the college.

On November 16, the South Carolina Human Affairs Commission issued a report on the incident. The report stated that a "minimal black representation" on the campus created "an environment lacking in ethnic diversity and cultural sensitivity." They recommended, among other things, that the school increase its black enrollment and add "mandatory human relations and cultural sensitivity classes" to the leadership training curriculum.

December 20-23. One black man was killed and two others were injured after a gang of white youths attacked them in the predominately white Howard Beach section of Queens, New York. Michael Griffith, a twenty-three-year-old construction worker from Brooklyn, was hit by a car and killed on a highway while attempting to escape his attackers. Another black man, Cedric Sandeford, age thirty-seven, was beaten with a baseball bat.

The three blacks had gone into a pizza parlor to call for help after their car broke down. According to police accounts, a gang of whites then confronted them, yelling racial slurs and asking, "What are you doing in this neighborhood?" The attack took place just outside the pizza parlor.

On December 23, three white teenagers were ordered held without bond on second-degree murder charges in connection with the attack. In an apparent act of revenge, a group of blacks in the Jamaica section of Queens chanted, "Howard Beach! Howard Beach!" while chasing and beating a white teenager who was walking to a bus stop. (Also see entries dated January 23, 1988; February 11, 1988; and December 11, 1989.)

1987 **January 17.** Ku Klux Klansmen and other white supremacists threw rocks and bottles at a group of ninety civil rights marchers in Forsyth County, Georgia. The 400 counter-demonstrators also shouted racial slurs at the marchers, who had gathered on a state road about two miles outside of the city of Cumming. There were no serious injuries, but eight of the supremacists were arrested on charges that included disorderly conduct, trespassing, and carrying a concealed weapon.

The would-be march was led by Dean Carter, a white martial arts instructor from Hall County, Georgia, and veteran civil rights leader Hosea Williams. Most of the participants were blacks from Atlanta, thirty miles south of Forsyth County. They had tried to get together once before for a "brotherhood walk" to honor the memory of Martin Luther King, Jr., but it was canceled after the organizers were threatened. (Also see entry dated January 24, 1987.)

January 24. More than 20,000 people, blacks as well as whites, marched for "brotherhood" and against racism in Forsyth County, Georgia. It was described as "the largest civil rights demonstration in two decades." Around 3,000 state and local police officers and National Guardsmen protected the marchers. There were a few minor injuries and sixty people, mostly white counter-demonstrators, were arrested.

The march was organized after a similar but much smaller protest a week earlier had been broken up by white counter-demonstrators who threw rocks and bottles. (See entry dated January 17, 1987.) Among the leaders of this new effort were Hosea Williams and Dean Carter, who had organized the original "brotherhood walk," as well as Coretta Scott King (widow of Martin Luther King, Jr.), Benjamin Hooks of the NAACP, and Joseph Lowery of the SCLC.

January 31. About 1,000 people rallied in Louisville, Kentucky, to protest the burning of a picture of slain civil rights leader Martin Luther King, Jr., by Ku Klux Klansmen. The demonstrators also condemned what they saw as an increase in racism and racist violence in the United States.

February 19-20. On February 19, about 200 blacks ran through the streets of Tampa, Florida, throwing rocks and setting fires. The disturbances began following the death of a twenty-three-year old black man. He had died after police tried to bring him under control by using a choke hold, which involves applying pressure to the main artery in the neck.

On February 20, isolated incidents of rock- and bottle-throwing continued, but there were no injuries. Two people were arrested. Meanwhile, black leaders and other volunteers walked the streets urging residents to remain calm.

Long before these outbreaks of violence, however, there had been other confrontations between blacks and law enforcement officers, including the death of another black man. Also, in December, 1986, New York Mets' star pitcher Dwight Gooden, an African American, had been arrested and charged with "battering police officers." A report by the city attorney later placed some of the blame for the Gooden incident on the police. The report also called on the city of Tampa to recruit more black police officers, since only 65 members of the 790-member police force were black. Local black leaders had complained for a long time about the lack of black police officers on the Tampa force.

February 26. Edgar Daniel "E.D." Nixon, "one of the fathers of the civil rights movement," died after surgery in Montgomery, Alabama, at the age of eighty-seven.

Nixon was born July 12, 1899, in Montgomery. He received only about sixteen months of formal education. Between 1923 and 1964, he worked as a Pullman porter on a Birmingham-to-Cincinnati train and was a longtime member of the Brotherhood of Sleeping Car Porters. In 1949, Nixon was elected president of the Alabama state NAACP.

Six years later, he was still active in the state and local NAACP when he received a call from Rosa Parks after she was arrested for refusing to give up her seat on a segregated Montgomery bus to a white man. When the local police refused to tell him anything about the situation because he was an "unauthorized person," Nixon contacted Clifford Durr, a white Montgomery lawyer sympathetic to blacks. Durr was able to find out the specific charge against Parks ("failing to obey a bus driver") and urged Nixon to seek the services of NAACP lawyer Fred D. Gray to challenge the constitutionality of the state law requiring segregation on city buses.

In addition to contacting Durr and Gray immediately after Parks's arrest, Nixon is also credited with posting her bail, informing Martin Luther King, Jr., of the incident, and proposing the Montgomery bus boycott. He also helped choose King as president of the Montgomery Improvement Association, the group that directed the successful 381-day boycott. (See entry dated December 1, 1955.)

Nixon is also known as the man who publicly scolded stubborn and fearful blacks into taking action in Montgomery. After some black ministers urged that the bus boycott be kept secret, Nixon asked, "What the heck you talking about? How you going to have a mass meeting, going to boycott a city bus line, without the white folk knowing it? You ought to make up your mind right now that you either admit you are a grown man or concede to the fact that you are a bunch of scared boys." He also told a crowd at a mass meeting, "Before you brothers and sisters get comfortable in your seats, I want to say if anybody here is afraid, he better take his hat and go home. We've worn aprons long enough. It's time for us to take them off."

Nixon's home, which was the target of a bomb during the height of the protests, is now an Alabama state historical landmark. Nixon himself was honored at a testimonial dinner in Atlanta, Georgia, in 1985. At that time, he remarked: "Fifty thousand people rose up and rocked the cradle of the Confederacy until we could sit where we wanted to on a bus.... A whole lot of things came about because we rocked the cradle."

August 24. Bayard Rustin, the African American civil rights activist who directed the 1963 March on Washington, died in New York City at the age of seventy-seven.

A native of West Chester, Pennsylvania, Rustin was born in March, 1910. An outstanding student and athlete, he graduated from high school with honors and went on to Cheyney State College and then Wilberforce College, where he studied literature and history. It was during this period that he also became interested in politics, which led him to join the Young Communist League in 1936.

Rustin left the League in 1941 and became a youth organizer for A. Philip Randolph's proposed July 1 March on Washington. (See entry dated June 25, 1941.) He was also an antiwar activist and spent more than two years in jail as a conscientious objector.

After his release in 1945, Rustin devoted himself to working on behalf of various peace programs, nuclear arms control, African independence movements, and, of course, the civil rights movement. He was active in the Congress of Racial Equality (CORE) as well as A. Philip Randolph's Committee against Discrimination in the Armed Forces. Later, during the 1950s, Rustin joined the Southern Christian Leadership Conference (SCLC).

In addition to being chief organizer of the 1963 March on Washington, Rustin was also responsible for many of the tactics and much of the strategy used by Martin

Luther King, Jr., and other leaders of the civil rights movement. During the 1960s and 1970s, he was often criticized by more "radical" blacks because he still supported nonviolent protest and advocated better education as the best means for blacks to gain racial equality. Yet Rustin continued to oppose nationalist and separatist ideas among African Americans. True to his peace-loving nature, he was also an early and outspoken opponent of American involvement in the Vietnam War.

At the time of his death, Rustin was co-chairman of the A. Philip Randolph Institute, a social-reform lobbying group. He had also just travelled to Cambodia and Haiti investigating reports of violence and injustice.

In its tribute to Rustin published on August 26, 1987, the *Atlanta Constitution* said that he "devoted his life to the fight for human rights, freedom and justice, not just in [the United States], but around the world.... His commitments to human rights and peace were neither trendy nor shallow.... America is indebted to Bayard Rustin. It is a better nation because of him."

October 27. Author and teacher John Oliver Killens died in New York City.

Killens was born in 1916 in Macon, Georgia. He left the South at the age of seventeen and lived most of the rest of his life in the North. He studied at Columbia University and New York University, then went to work for the National Labor Relations Board in Washington, D.C. He returned to his job there after serving in the military during World War II.

Killens was an original member of the Harlem Writers Guild and worked on Paul Robeson's newspaper, *Freedom*. He also taught creative writing at Fisk, Columbia, and Howard universities, earning a reputation for opening his home at night to students "for talk, food, and sometimes, shelter."

Killens is known to have inspired a generation of young black writers, including Wesley Brown, Nikki Giovanni, Richard Perry, Janet Tolliver, and Brenda Wilkinson. His own philosophy was that "the responsibility of the writer is to take the facts and deepen them into eternal truth. Every time I sit down to the typewriter, put pen to paper," he once said, "I'm out to change the world."

Killens' major novels included *Youngblood* (1954), *And Then We Heard the Thunder* (1963), and *The Cotillion; or, One Good Bull Is Half the Herd* (1971). *Youngblood* was a story of "powerful courage" among ordinary black folks in a small Georgia town, while *The Cotillion* was a "hilarious satire [of] social-climbing" black northerners.

Some critics contended that Killens's later works "lacked the power" of his first two novels, *Youngblood* and *And Then We Heard the Thunder*. But at least one reviewer, Tina McElroy Ansa, declared that if literary historians are looking for the quality of "power ... they should also look to the man. There, they will find the power they seek. The power of his teaching, the power of his courage, the power of his generosity, the power of his gentleness, the power of his example, the power of his life."

Like many other blacks who left the South in the first half of the twentieth century, Killens was always reluctant to go back to his own native region. His first extended visit to his hometown occurred in 1986, when he spent two weeks there as a lecturer and writer-in-residence.

November 25. Harold Washington, the first African American mayor of Chicago, Illinois, died of an apparent heart attack. He was six months into his second term as mayor when he collapsed while working in his City Hall office.

Washington was first elected mayor of Chicago in 1983 after a bitter contest with strong racial overtones. He won reelection in April, 1987, by campaigning on a theme of "uniting the city's diverse racial and ethnic groups." His first term was marred by racial divisions between black and white aldermen and by opposition to his policies among white ethnics on the city council. (See entry dated February 23, 1983.)

The Chicago City Council later elected Eugene Sawyer, an African American, to serve as acting mayor until new elections could be held. (Also see entry dated February 28, 1989.)

December 1. James Baldwin, African American writer and civil rights activist, died of cancer at his home in St. Paul de Vence, France, at the age of sixty-three. Baldwin had moved to France in 1948 to escape what he felt was "the stifling racial bigotry" of the United States.

The son of a preacher, Baldwin was born in the Harlem section of New York City in 1924. He began writing while he was a student at the DeWitt Clinton High School in the Bronx. By the time he was in his early twenties, he was publishing essays and reviews in such publications as the *Nation,* the *New Leader, Commentary,* and

James Baldwin

Partisan Review. During this same period, Baldwin also became friends with a number of New York writers and intellectuals, including William Barrett, Irving Howe, and Lionel Trilling.

Baldwin was a very productive author. Most of his work focused on sexual identity and racial tension in a world dominated by whites. He published his three most important collections of essays—*Notes of a Native Son* (1955), *Nobody Knows My Name* (1961), and *The Fire Next Time* (1963)—during the height of the civil rights movement. Other important works by Baldwin include the novel *Go Tell It on the Mountain* (1953), which was his first book; *Giovanni's Room* (1956) and *Another Country* (1962), which contain frank discussions of homosexuality; and the drama *Blues for Mister Charlie* (1964). According to the author, this last book was inspired "very distantly" by the 1955 lynching of Emmett Till, a black youth in Mississippi. (See entry dated August 28, 1955.)

During the civil rights movement, Baldwin not only wrote about the struggle, he also helped raise money for it and organized protest marches. In addition, he was an early opponent of the American involvement in the Vietnam War and a critic of discrimination against homosexuals.

Baldwin's writings and activism were recognized by many groups both in this country and abroad. In 1986, for example, he received the distinguished Legion of Honor, France's highest national award.

December 15. Septima Poinsetta Clark, African American educator and civil rights activist, died on John's Island, South Carolina, at the age of eighty-nine.

Clark was born to a former slave in Charleston, South Carolina, in 1898. She received a bachelor's degree from Benedict College in her native state and a master's from Hampton Institute in Virginia. She returned to South Carolina and began her teaching career in a public school on John's Island in 1916. In 1918, she transferred to Avery Institute in Charleston.

That same year, Clark led a drive to collect 20,000 signatures on a petition to have black teachers hired by the Charleston County School District. The law barring their employment was finally changed in 1920.

Seven years later, after she moved to Columbia, Clark helped with a campaign to equalize salaries for black and white teachers. She eventually moved back to Charleston, where school officials fired her from her teaching job in 1955 for being a member of the National Association for the Advancement of Colored People (NAACP).

During the late 1950s, Clark worked at the Highlander Folk School in Tennessee. There she developed a program to teach blacks how to read so that they could pass literacy tests and qualify to vote. She later became a director of the school, a supervisor of teacher training for the Southern Christian Leadership Conference (SCLC), and a national lecturer for voting and civil rights. In 1974, she was elected to the Charleston County School Board.

In recognition of her contributions to the civil rights movement, Martin Luther King, Jr., asked Clark to accompany him to Norway in 1964 when he received the Nobel Peace Prize. In 1979, President Jimmy Carter presented Clark with a Living Legacy Award. And in 1982, she received the Order of the Palmetto, South Carolina's highest civilian award.

Clark told the story of much of her life in her autobiographies, *Echo in My Soul* (1962) and *Ready from Within: Septima Clark and the Civil Rights Movement* (1987). The latter won an American Book Award.

1988   **January 18.** Political, civil rights, and religious leaders throughout the nation led celebrations of the third national holiday in honor of civil rights leader Dr. Martin Luther King, Jr. As of 1988, forty-three states observed the national King holiday. Only Arizona, Hawaii, Idaho, Montana, New Hampshire, South Dakota, and Wyoming continued to refuse to recognize the event.

In Phoenix, Arizona, thousands marched through the downtown area demanding that the King holiday be restored. In 1987, Governor Evan Meacham had repealed the state's observance of the holiday. This action was the first of many that led to an effort to remove him from office. (Also see entries dated November 6, 1990; January, 1992; and January 18, 1993.)

January 23. Jon Lester, a white teenager, was sentenced in New York City to serve a prison term of ten to thirty years for his part in the December 20, 1986, beating death of Michael Griffith, a black man.

The attack in the predominantly white neighborhood of Howard Beach in the Queens section of New York City had inflamed racial tensions and prompted several days of protest demonstrations led by the clergyman Al Sharpton. Lester was the first of three convicted white teenagers to be sentenced. (Also see entries dated December 20-23, 1986; February 11, 1988; and December 11, 1989.)

January 31. The *Atlanta Journal-Constitution* reported the results of a poll that showed 75 percent of Alabama's white residents wanted to keep flying the Confederate flag over the state capitol at Montgomery.

In December, 1987, the Alabama NAACP announced a campaign to remove the flag from the statehouse. The organization's state director, Thomas Reed, said he would climb the flagpole and tear it down himself. Yet Alabama governor Guy Hunt insisted that the flag would continue to fly unless a majority of Alabamians wanted it removed.

As of 1988, Alabama and South Carolina were the only two southern states that officially continued to fly the Confederate flag. Mississippi and Georgia included the Confederate symbol as part of their state flags. From time to time, some blacks in these states have protested the use of the Confederate symbol by public agencies and institutions. They maintain that its identification with the pro-slavery states in the American Civil War make it a racist emblem. (Also see entries dated December 12, 1992, and January, 1993.)

January 31. Doug Williams, the African American quarterback of the Washington Redskins, was named the Most Valuable Player of Super Bowl XXII.

A graduate of predominantly black Grambling University in Louisiana, Williams was the first black quarterback ever to start in a Super Bowl championship game. He completed 18 of 29 passes totaling 340 yards and four touchdowns. The Redskins defeated the Denver Broncos of the American Football Conference 42-10.

February 11. Jason Ladone, age seventeen, became the second white teenager to be sentenced to prison for his part in the December 20, 1986, beating death of a young black man, Michael Griffith, in the Howard Beach section of Queens in New York City.

Ladone received a term of five to fifteen years for manslaughter and assault. He was the only defendant in the case to plead for mercy and the only one to apologize to the victim's mother, Jean Griffith. (Also see entries dated December 20-23, 1986; January 23, 1988; and December 11, 1989.)

February 19. Several hundred students at the University of Massachusetts at Amherst held a demonstration against racism at the institution. They were showing their support for an agreement that had just been reached between minorities and the school's administration after a six-day takeover of a campus building. The demonstrators also called on students to skip classes for two days beginning March 22 to denounce racism, sexism, and an alleged attack against three Puerto Rican students on February 17.

Racial tensions on campus had increased after at least 200 black, American Indian, and Hispanic students took over the New Africa House on February 12 to protest alleged assaults and racial slurs by white students. They left the building on February 17 after the school's chancellor promised to expel students who repeatedly committed acts of racial violence. The chancellor also agreed to promote multicultural education. (Also see entry dated October 6, 1992.)

February 20. Attorneys for Boston University asked a Suffolk (Massachusetts) Superior Court judge to order Coretta Scott King to release tapes of conversations between her late husband, Dr. Martin Luther King, Jr., and others that had been secretly recorded by federal investigators. (See entries dated November 19, 1975; May 29-June 3, 1978; and November 17, 1978.) The attorneys also asked for the release of correspondence between King and his colleagues.

This action was the latest round in a legal battle between the school and Mrs. King over an estimated 83,000 documents relating to her husband that are held at Boston University. Mrs. King had filed suit earlier, claiming that the documents belonged in the Martin Luther King, Jr., Center for Non-Violent Social Change in Atlanta, Georgia. She also declared that the university had "mishandled or lost some of the papers." (Also see entry dated May 6, 1993.)

March 5. Governor Michael Dukakis of Massachusetts moved closer to winning the Democratic nomination for president of the United States after a major victory over his African American rival, the reverend Jesse Jackson, in the Wisconsin primary.

March 12. Jesse Jackson, African American candidate for the Democratic party's presidential nomination, won precinct caucuses in the state of South Carolina. Kevin Gray, Jackson's campaign manager in South Carolina, estimated that his candidate would eventually be awarded about 25 of the 44 national convention delegates at stake in the South Carolina vote.

Although Jackson was a resident of Chicago, Illinois, he was a native of Greenville, South Carolina, and had "the status of a favorite son." He also had the almost solid support of the South's second largest black population. A minister, he had a campaign organization that worked hard with the state's 4,000 black churches to turn out the vote.

March 15. Pope John Paul II appointed fifty-three-year-old Eugene Antonio Marino, a black Josephite priest, as the archbishop of Atlanta, Georgia. It was the first time that an African American had been named an archbishop in the American Roman Catholic Church.

A native of Biloxi, Mississippi, Marino studied at St. Joseph's Seminary in Washington, D.C., from 1956 to 1962 and earned a master's degree in religious education from Fordham University. From 1962 to 1968, he taught in and directed training activities in the archdiocese of Washington, D.C. On July 13, 1971, Marino was elected to a four-year term as vicar general of the Josephite Fathers.

Before becoming archbishop of Atlanta, Marino was the auxiliary bishop of Washington, D.C., and secretary of the National Conference of Catholic Bishops. He was one of only twelve black bishops in the United States at the time Pope John II promoted him to archbishop.

In his new position, Marino became the spiritual leader of 156,000 Roman Catholics (10,000 of whom were blacks) in sixty-nine counties in northern Georgia. Most of them were members of seven churches (including three predominantly black ones) in the city of Atlanta. (Also see entry dated July, 1990.)

March 16. President Ronald Reagan vetoed a civil rights bill that was designed to reverse a 1984 U.S. Supreme Court decision and restore the impact of four federal laws that banned discrimination on the basis of race, age, handicap, or sex. The high Court had ruled in 1984 that federal law prohibiting racial discrimination by schools and colleges extends only to the affected program or activity, not to the entire institution. (See entries dated February 28, 1984; March 20, 1988; and March 22, 1988.)

Reagan objected to the bill (known as the Civil Rights Restoration Act) because he felt it gave the federal government too much power to interfere with and control the affairs of state and local governments, businesses, and church-related institutions. Instead, he offered an alternative—a slight expansion on a previous version that had been rejected in both houses of Congress—that he said would "protect civil rights and at the same time preserve the independence of state and local governments, the freedom of religion, and the right of America's citizens to order their lives and businesses without extensive federal intrusion."

March 16. After finishing second in the Democratic presidential primary in Illinois on March 15, African American presidential candidate Jesse Jackson had won an estimated 460.5 delegates. Jackson's total placed him just four delegates behind the Democratic frontrunner, Massachusetts governor Michael Dukakis, who had 464.5 delegates at the time. (A candidate needed a total of 2,082 votes to capture the Democratic nomination.) With almost half of the Democratic delegates chosen by this date, Jackson had won more popular votes than any other Democratic contender.

March 20. The U.S. House of Representatives voted to overturn a U.S. Supreme Court ruling that had limited four laws banning discrimination based on age, race, sex, or handicap. The U.S. Senate had approved the same measure on January 28.

The legislation, known as the Civil Rights Restoration Act, requires that any institution receiving federal funds (including school systems, corporations, and health facilities) must comply with civil rights laws. It allows limited exemptions for small businesses, churches, farmers who receive federal price supports, and welfare recipients. (Also see entries dated February 28, 1984; March 16, 1988; and March 22, 1988.)

March 20. In Tokyo, Japan, twenty-one-year-old boxer Mike Tyson knocked out challenger Tony Tubbs to retain the world heavyweight championship.

March 22. The U.S. Congress overrode President Ronald Reagan's veto of the Civil Rights Restoration Act. (Also see entries dated February 28, 1984; March 16, 1988; and March 20, 1988.)

March 31. African American novelist Toni Morrison won a Pulitzer Prize for Fiction for her book *Beloved*. Set in Ohio after the end of the Civil War, the novel revolves around the painful, horror-filled memories of a former slave.

Morrison was born in Lorain, Ohio, in 1931. She received her bachelor's degree from Howard University in 1953 and her master's degree from Cornell University in 1955. After teaching for a few years, first at Texas Southern University and then at Howard University, she went to work as an editor for Random House. In her spare time, Morrison also took up writing to help her cope with the loneliness of her life as a single mother of two young sons.

In 1970, Morrison published her first novel, *The Bluest Eye*. Although it was not especially popular with critics or readers, a second novel, *Sula,* was very well received when it appeared in 1973. She followed it up with the highly successful novels *Song of Solomon* (1977) and *Tar Baby* (1981), both of which were award-winning bestsellers.

Toni Morrison

Beloved came next. It provoked a controversy in the fall of 1987 when it failed to win the prestigious National Book Award. In January, 1988, forty-eight black writers wrote an open letter to the *New York Times Book Review* to protest that oversight as well as the fact that Morrison had never won the even more prestigious Pulitzer Prize.

Responding to the announcement of the award, Morrison said, "I think I know what I feel.... I had no doubt about the value of the book and that it was really worth serious recognition. But I had some dark thoughts about whether the book's merits would be allowed to be the only consideration of the Pulitzer committee. The book had begun to take on a responsibility, an extra-literary responsibility, that it was never designed for."

Beloved cemented Morrison's reputation as one of today's most highly regarded black women writers. In nearly all her work, she draws heavily from black folklore and black storytelling traditions to create vivid female characters in language known for its poetic beauty.

June 5. Clarence M. Pendleton, Jr., chairman of the U.S. Civil Rights Commission (CCR), died of an apparent heart attack in San Diego, California, at the age of fifty-seven.

During the late 1970s, while he was head of the San Diego Urban League, Pendleton was the only one of more than 150 officers in the League to support the presidential candidacy of former California governor Ronald Reagan. By 1980, he had abandoned what he called his "bleeding-heart liberalism" and switched to the Republican party.

In 1981, President Reagan appointed him to be the first black chairman of the CCR. (See entry dated November 16, 1981.) As chairman, Pendleton led the CCR toward a "color-blind" approach to civil rights. He opposed busing to achieve school desegregation and called affirmative action a "bankrupt policy." Civil rights leaders, some political figures, and even some members of the CCR itself expressed shock at the positions he took on some issues. Congress responded by drastically cutting the CCR's budget. These cuts greatly slowed down the activity at the CCR.

July 13. As the date for the 1988 Democratic National Convention approached, Massachusetts governor Michael Dukakis had won enough delegate votes to win his party's nomination over his closest rival, the African American candidate Jesse Jackson. However, some Democrats wondered if Jackson and his followers might try to disrupt the convention. There were also some fears about whether they would enthusiastically support the party's candidate in the November elections because of tensions between the Jackson and Dukakis camps.

July 19. Jesse Jackson, African American Democratic presidential candidate, electrified listeners with a speech at the Democratic National Convention in Atlanta, Georgia, on the eve of the voting for the presidential nomination. His remarks focused on the theme of "Keep Hope Alive."

July 20. The quest of Jesse Jackson for the Democratic nomination for president of the United States ended in Atlanta, Georgia. Delegates at the Democratic National Convention there gave the party's nomination to Massachusetts governor Michael Dukakis. The number of delegates needed for nomination was 2,082. Dukakis won with 2,876.25 delegate votes; Jackson came in second with 1,218.5 votes.

Jackson had begun his second attempt to win the Democratic nomination shortly after he failed to do so in 1984. Through his organizations Operation PUSH and the Rainbow Coalition, he was an outspoken supporter of the civil rights of blacks, other minorities, and women. More recently, he had also taken up the causes of labor and farmers who were facing hard times.

Unlike his race in 1984, when several major black leaders publicly opposed his candidacy, Jackson was able to win their support or at least their neutrality in his latest campaign. He was also able to persuade more whites to back his candidacy. He ran as a populist, or someone who supports the cause of ordinary people who feel they are not getting their fair share of the nation's political, social, and economic opportunities.

In the primary elections and caucuses held before the Democratic National Convention, Jackson won the votes of 92 percent of blacks and 12 percent of whites. Four years earlier he had captured 77 percent of the black vote, but only 5 percent of the white vote.

Jackson's achievements in the 1988 campaign established him as the most formidable black candidate ever to seek the American presidency.

July 31. Forty-seven-year-old Willie Stargell, a former African American baseball star with the Pittsburgh Pirates of the National Baseball League, was inducted into the Baseball Hall of Fame in ceremonies at Cooperstown, New York. He was the first player to be selected on his first try since Lou Brock, another African American, accomplished the feat in 1985.

Jesse Jackson prepares to speak at the 1988 Democratic National Convention

Stargell's best seasons as a baseball player were in 1971, when he scored 48 home runs, batted in 125 runs, and had a total batting average of .295; and in 1973, when he hit 44 home runs, batted in 119 runs, and ended with a batting average of .299. Stargell played in the 1971 and 1979 World Series and was named the Most Valuable Player in the 1979 Series.

August 11. M. Carl Holman, president of the National Urban Coalition, died of cancer in Washington, D.C., at the age of sixty-nine.

Holman was born June 27, 1919, in Minter, Mississippi, but grew up in St. Louis, Missouri. He graduated with top honors from Lincoln University, then earned master's degrees at the University of Chicago in 1944 and Yale University in 1954. Between the time he received his two master's degrees, Holman taught English at Hampton Institute and Lincoln University. Beginning in 1949, he launched a long career in Georgia as a professor of English at Clark College.

While in Georgia, Holman was an advisor to the student sit-in movement in Atlanta. In 1961, he helped escort and protect Charlayne Hunter and Hamilton Holmes when the two black students desegregated the University of Georgia. He was also editor of the *Atlanta Inquirer,* a black weekly newspaper, which was founded as a voice for civil rights demonstrators.

In 1962, Holman left Clark College to become information officer and later deputy staff director of the U.S. Civil Rights Commission (CCR) from 1962 to 1968. He then became a vice-president of the National Urban Coalition, a group that studies social and economic life in American cities and works to find ways to help them survive and succeed. Holman was named president of the Coalition in 1971.

August 27. More than 55,000 Americans marched in Washington, D.C., to commemorate the twenty-fifth anniversary of the historic 1963 March on Washington. (See entry dated August 28, 1963.) The leaders of the new march included Democratic presidential candidates Jesse Jackson and Michael Dukakis, Benjamin Hooks of the NAACP, Coretta Scott King (widow of slain civil rights leader Martin Luther King, Jr.), and Joseph Lowery of the SCLC.

The themes of the gathering were a tribute to Martin Luther King, Jr., and his famous "I Have a Dream" speech as well as a protest against the civil rights policies of the Reagan administration. In addressing the latter topic, the SCLC's Lowery told the crowd, "We fought too long, we prayed too hard, we wept too bitterly, we bled too profusely, we died too young to let anybody ever turn back the clock on racial justice. We ain't going back."

September 26. A seven-month-long grand jury investigation in New York State concluded that Tawana Brawley, a sixteen-year-old African American, had made up her story about being kidnapped and sexually abused by a gang of white men in Wyspingers Falls, New York, on November 24, 1987.

Brawley had disappeared from her home four days earlier. She was found nude in a garbage bag with feces and racial slurs covering her body. Within days, her case became a focal point of protests and racial tensions throughout the state. Al Sharpton, a clergyman and community activist, and lawyers Alton H. Maddox, Jr., and C. Vernon Mason were among the leaders of the protests and also served as advisors to Brawley. The three told the Brawley family not to cooperate with police, whom they accused of a cover-up in the case. The group even charged that law enforcement officials were involved in the alleged attack on Brawley.

Nevertheless, the grand jury's final report found "no evidence of any abduction, racial or sexual attack, or any other crime against Miss Brawley."

September 26. The International Olympic Committee (IOC) took away Canadian Ben Johnson's gold medal in the 100-meter dash after he tested positive for "performance-enhancing anabolic steroids." The medal, which he had won in the Summer Olympic Games at Seoul, South Korea, on September 24, was then presented to the second place finisher in the 100-meter dash, African American Carl Lewis.

October 3. *Forbes Magazine* reported that Michael Jackson, a thirty-year-old African American, had become the world's highest-paid entertainer. The magazine estimated his 1988 income at $60 million, about $40 million of which he made during a worldwide tour. The rest of his earnings came from sales of his album *Bad*, his autobiography *Moonwalk*, music publishing, and endorsements and commercials he made for the Pepsi Cola Bottling company.

Just the year before, the wealthiest entertainer was another African American, comedian Bill Cosby. He had an estimated income in 1986-87 of $84 million. Other African Americans on the 1988 list were actor-comedian Eddie Murphy, talk show host Oprah Winfrey, and professional boxers Mike Tyson, Sugar Ray Leonard, and Michael Spinks.

October 26. S.B. Fuller, founder and president of Fuller Products Company and a "dean of black entrepreneurs," died of kidney failure in Blue Island, Illinois, at age eighty-three.

Fuller was a native of Ouachita Parish, Louisiana. He left school after the sixth grade and lived in poverty until his mother, who died when he was seventeen, convinced him to become a door-to-door salesman. He sold cosmetics and built a national company with more than 5,000 salesmen.

During the 1960s, Fuller expanded his company into newspapers, appliance and department stores, as well as farming and beef cattle production. He is credited with teaching business skills to John H. Johnson, founder of the highly successful Johnson Publishing Company, and George Johnson, one of the nation's leading cosmetics manufacturers.

November 4. Comedian and television star Bill Cosby announced his intention to donate $20 million to Spelman College, an institution for African American women in Atlanta, Georgia. It was the largest single gift in the 107-year history of the college and the largest such gift ever made by an African American. In announcing the donation, Cosby urged other blacks to do more in supporting historically black colleges. "I think we all understand that schools need money, but I think we accepted that white folks were going to keep them alive."

November 4. Dedication of the Martin Luther King, Jr., Federal Building was held in Atlanta, Georgia. U.S. congressman John Lewis and members of the slain civil rights leader's family participated in the ceremonies. Lewis had sponsored the bill in Congress to rename the building for King, the first federal building in the nation to bear his name.

November 8. Vice-President George Bush, running as the Republican candidate for president, easily defeated Democrat Michael Dukakis with a promise "to make kinder the face of the nation and gentler the face of the world."

December 20. Forty-nine-year-old Max Robinson, the first black news anchorman on American network television, died of complications from AIDS in Washington, D.C.

Robinson, who had worked as a news anchor at WTOP-TV in Washington, became a co-anchor with Peter Jennings and Frank Reynolds on ABC's "Evening News" in 1978. But Carl Bernstein, chief of the ABC News bureau in Chicago, Illinois, said Robinson was "deliberately excluded from any decision-making related to the newscast." In a speech at Smith College in February, 1981, Robinson accused ABC of racism. Two years later, after the death of Frank Reynolds, Jennings was named sole anchor of the "Evening News." Robinson was then assigned to anchor on weekends and do news briefs. The next year he left ABC and joined WMAQ-TV in Chicago.

In June, 1985, Robinson entered a hospital suffering from "emotional and physical exhaustion." He never returned to full-time news reporting.

December 28. Widespread discussion began in African American communities throughout the United States over the proper ethnic name for Americans of African origin.

Former Democratic presidential candidate Jesse Jackson, leaders of the NAACP, and others had agreed during a conference in Chicago that "African American" should replace "black," which gained prominence during the civil rights movement of the 1960s. Jackson said the term African American "[places] us in our proper historical context." Others disagreed, including the clergyman B. Herbert Martin, head of the Human Relations Commission in Chicago, Illinois. He said the change from "black to African-American amounted to little more than semantics." (Also see entry dated January 29, 1991.)

1989   **January 23.** The U.S. Supreme Court ruled unconstitutional a program in Richmond, Virginia, that required contractors in city construction projects to "set aside" at least 30 percent "of the value of the project" for companies "at least half-minority owned." The Court said that "the quota" was "an unlawful form of reverse discrimination."

The decision was one of the most far-reaching attacks on the idea of affirmative action since the *Regents of University of California v. Allan Bakke* decision in 1978. (Also see entries dated June 25, 1976; June 28, 1978; June 12, 1984; and June 12, 1989.)

January 24. Officials of the U.S. Episcopal Church approved the election of Barbara Harris, a fifty-eight-year-old African American, as the first female bishop in history and scheduled her ordination for February 11, 1989.

Harris was born and raised in Philadelphia, Pennsylvania. She worked in the business world as a public relations specialist for nearly thirty years before she decided in the mid-1970s to study for the priesthood. (The Episcopal Church had just voted to ap-

Barbara Harris

prove women as priests.) In 1980, Harris achieved her goal when she was ordained an Episcopal priest after completing her education through correspondence courses and with tutors.

Harris then served as a part-time priest in a Philadelphia church and as a prison chaplain. In 1984, she became the executive director of the Episcopal Church Publishing Company, where she attracted national attention as columnist, editor, and publisher of *The Witness,* a church journal with a reputation for supporting various liberal causes. (Harris herself was a longtime political and social activist.) She remained in that position until 1988, when she was chosen to serve as temporary head of the Church of the Advocate, an inner-city Episcopal parish in Philadelphia.

At a church conference later that same year, a group of Episcopal bishops from around the world reluctantly approved the idea of allowing women to serve as bishops. Some liberal clergymen from the United States immediately nominated Harris to fill the position of suffragan (assistant) bishop in the diocese of Boston, Massachusetts. On September 24, 1988, she overcame tremendous opposition from many conservative churchmen to defeat five other candidates—three white men, a black man, and a white woman. Her election thus ended the 2,000-year-old tradition of male bishops that dated back to Jesus and his apostles.

February 10. Ron Brown was elected chairman of the Democratic National Committee, making him the first black to lead a major American political party. He had previously served as Jesse Jackson's campaign manager during the 1988 presidential campaign.

February 24. President George Bush named William Lucas, an African American attorney from Detroit, Michigan, assistant attorney general for civil rights. This appointment also made him director of the Civil Rights Division of the Department of Justice.

Conservative groups praised Lucas's appointment, but civil rights organizations expressed some concerns. They pointed out that he opposed quotas to help minorities and that he had not worked on civil rights matters at the federal level for at least twenty years. (Also see entry dated August 1, 1989.)

February 25. In Las Vegas, Nevada, Mike Tyson retained his heavyweight boxing championship by knocking out British fighter Frank Bruno in the fifth round of a scheduled 15-round bout.

February 28. Richard M. Daley defeated acting mayor Eugene Sawyer in the Democratic primary election for mayor of Chicago, Illinois. Daley, the son of legendary Chicago mayor Richard J. Daley, captured 57 percent of the vote, compared to 43 percent for the African American Sawyer. The vote was "marked by a sharp split along racial lines," but voter turnout in the black wards of the city was lower than usual.

As a result of the primary, the general election scheduled for April 11, 1989, was to be decided among three candidates: Daley, Republican Alderman Edward R. Vrdolyak (who, like Daley, is white), and black independent Timothy C. Evans. The winner of that election would serve the final two years of the late Harold Washington's term in office. (Also see entry dated November 25, 1987.)

March 6. Richmond Barthe, a prominent African American sculptor and member of the National Academy of Arts and Letters, died at his home in Pasadena, California. He was eighty-eight years old.

Born in 1901 in Bay St. Louis, Mississippi, Barthe studied at the Chicago Art Institute from 1924 until 1928. At first he was drawn to painting but then switched to sculpture when some of his experimental pieces attracted the attention of art critics. His work was eventually featured in a number of exhibitions at major American museums, including the Metropolitan Museum of Art in New York City. Among his most famous works are *Singing Slave, Maurice Evans,* and *Henry O. Tanner.*

March 10. The U.S. Senate confirmed Dr. Louis Sullivan, president of the Morehouse School of Medicine in Atlanta, Georgia, as the new Secretary of Health and Human Services (HHS).

The confirmation followed more than two months of heated controversy regarding Sullivan's beliefs on abortion. At first, he declared himself to be pro-choice, which put him at odds with the strongly pro-life Bush administration. Sullivan then began to back away from this position, saying that he was opposed to abortion except in cases of rape or incest or to save the mother's life. Finally, when he testified before the Senate, he confessed that he "misspoke" earlier when he said he supported a woman's right to an abortion. He was confirmed the next month.

March 16. The U.S. Senate voted to try U.S. District Court Judge Alcee Hastings on charges of fraud, corruption, and perjury in connection with a 1981 bribery conspiracy case for which he had been acquitted in 1983. The Senate created a special 12-member committee to hear testimony and collect evidence. If found guilty of misconduct, Hastings faced removal from office.

The fifty-three-year-old Hastings was appointed to the federal bench in 1979 by President Jimmy Carter. He was the first African American ever to serve in this position in the state of Florida. (Also see entries dated October 20, 1989, and November 3, 1992.)

April 1. Bill White was elected president of the National Baseball League, making him the first African American ever to head a major professional sports league in the United States.

A six-time All-Star first baseman, White played with the St. Louis Cardinals, the Philadelphia Phillies, and the New York and San Francisco Giants between 1956 and 1969. At the time of his appointment, he was a television announcer for the New York Yankees of the American Baseball League and a broadcaster with CBS Radio.

April 3. Twenty students occupied and barricaded the administration building at predominantly black Morris Brown College in Atlanta, Georgia. The demonstrators' demands included "a more lenient delinquent fees policy, a Pan-African studies program, better campus services (including a new cafeteria vendor) and (after a recent dormitory fire), an upgraded physical plant."

The Morris Brown demonstration followed similar recent student takeovers at historically black Howard University in Washington, D.C., and predominantly white Wayne State University in Detroit, Michigan.

May 22. Television talk-show host Oprah Winfrey, an African American, received a Doctor of Humane Letters degree from Morehouse College in Atlanta, Georgia, and gave the prestigious all-male school a gift of $1 million. She requested that the money be used to establish a scholarship fund to educate at least 100 black men in the coming decades.

Winfrey's gift represented a growing trend among black entertainers and athletes to lend their support to America's financially impoverished black colleges. Other recent donations included comedian Bill Cosby's gifts of $800,000 to Meharry Medical College, $325,000 to Howard University, $1.3 million to Fisk University, and $20 million to Spelman College; singer Lionel Richie's gift of $500,000 to Tuskegee University; and singer Michael Jackson's gift of $600,000 to the United Negro College Fund (UNCF).

May 24. President George Bush met with seventeen members of the Congressional Black Caucus (CBC). It was the first time since 1981 that the Caucus, which had been critical of the civil rights policies of former President Ronald Reagan, was invited to the White House.

June 7. Joan Salmon Campbell, a fifty-year-old African American from Philadelphia, Pennsylvania, was elected head of the Presbyterian Church, U.S.A. She was the sixth female and the first black woman to lead the church.

June 12. The U.S. Supreme Court ruled that workers "who are adversely affected by court-approved affirmative action plans may file lawsuits alleging discrimination."

This opened the door for white workers to file reverse discrimination lawsuits against large employers who had been trying to follow the law and correct past examples of discrimination against minorities. (Also see entries dated June 25, 1976; June 28, 1978; June 12, 1984; and January 23, 1989.)

June 26. Two of the nation's oldest black institutions of higher education, Atlanta University (founded in 1867) and Clark College (founded in 1869), merged to form a new institution known as Clark-Atlanta University. It was created in response to severe financial problems at Atlanta University and a shortage of classroom space and research facilities at Clark College.

July 10. African American businessmen Bertram Lee of Boston, Massachusetts, and Peter Bynoe of Chicago, Illinois, purchased the Denver Nuggets of the National Basketball Association, becoming the first blacks ever to own a professional sports franchise.

July 21. In Atlantic City, New Jersey, African American heavyweight boxing champion Mike Tyson knocked out Carl "The Truth" Williams in the first minute and a half of their fight to retain his world title.

August 1. The Senate Judiciary Committee rejected the nomination of African American attorney William Lucas for the post of U.S. Assistant Attorney General. If he had been confirmed, Lucas would have headed the civil rights division of the U.S. Justice Department.

Some legislators and civil rights leaders pointed to his inexperience, his opposition to racial quotas in employment, and his support of recent Supreme Court decisions that severely limited affirmative action programs as the reasons behind the rejection. (Also see entry dated February 24, 1989.)

August 7-13. On August 7, an airplane with black congressman Mickey Leland aboard crashed en route to a refugee camp in the African nation of Ethiopia. On August 13, searchers discovered the bodies of Leland and fifteen others who had been on board the plane with him.

The forty-four-year-old Leland represented Texas in Congress. At the time of his death, he was chairman of the House Select Committee on Hunger. He had made six previous trips to Africa to investigate and draw attention to famine conditions, particularly in war-torn Ethiopia.

August 10. Army General Colin Powell was named chairman of the U.S. Joint Chiefs of Staff, the highest military position in the country. The fifty-two-year-old Powell was the first African American and also the youngest man ever to serve as chairman of the joint chiefs.

Powell, the son of West Indian immigrants, was born in the Harlem section of New York City on April 5, 1937. He received a bachelor's degree from the City College of New York in 1958 and then was commissioned a second lieutenant in the Army. (He later earned a master's degree in business administration from George Washington University in 1971 and attended the National War College in 1975-76.) Powell then began a steady rise through the ranks. He served two tours of duty in Vietnam during the 1960s, first as an advisor to the Vietnamese army in 1962-63 and later as an infantry officer in 1968-69.

During the 1970s and early 1980s, Powell held a variety of military jobs throughout the United States and Europe and political appointments in Washington, D.C. Perhaps his most important post was as

Colin Powell visits an air base in Saudi Arabia during the Persian Gulf War

deputy assistant and later assistant to President Ronald Reagan for national security affairs during the late 1980s. In that role, Powell was credited with helping restore the tarnished image of the National Security Council (NSC) after the Iran-Contra scandal.

Promoted to full general in 1989, Powell then left the capital to become commander in chief of Forces Command at Fort McPherson, Georgia. Then came the call from President George Bush to return to Washington as chairman of the Joint Chiefs. (Also see entry dated September 20, 1989.)

August 21. Fifteen people, including a four-month-old baby girl, were injured when a package exploded in the southeast regional offices of the NAACP in Atlanta, Georgia. The injuries, mostly eye irritations and congestion, resulted from a tear-gas bomb but were not considered serious. (Also see entry dated December 16-20, 1989.)

August 22. Huey Newton, a co-founder of the Black Panther Party, was shot to death in Oakland, California. He was forty-seven years old.

Since giving up his racial activism in the late 1960s, Newton had continued to have trouble with the law. In 1974, for example, he was charged with pistol-whipping his tailor, possessing a handgun, and murdering a seventeen-year-old prostitute. Before he could go to trial on the murder charges, however, Newton fled to Cuba. He returned in 1977 and was tried twice for murder. But both ended in mistrials with the juries deadlocked in favor of acquittal. The murder charges were finally dismissed in 1979.

Meanwhile, in 1978, Newton was convicted of possessing a handgun but was acquitted on the charge of assaulting his tailor after the man refused to testify against him. Newton served nine months in California's San Quentin Prison on the gun charge in 1987. In March, 1989, he was sentenced to six months in jail after pleading no contest to charges of taking $15,000 in public funds that had been given to the Black Panthers for a school they had operated in the early 1980s.

In between his legal scrapes, Newton had earned a doctorate degree in social philosophy from the University of California at Santa Cruz in 1980. At the time of his death, he was trying to overcome drug and alcohol problems. The man accused of killing Newton was a known drug dealer who claimed he had shot the former

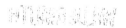

Panther in self-defense. (Also see entries dated September 8, 1968; May 29, 1970; August, 1970; August 8, 1971; December 15, 1971; and November 2, 1974.)

August 23. Yusef Hawkins, a sixteen-year-old African American youth, was shot to death in the predominantly white Bensonhurst section of Brooklyn, New York. Hawkins and three friends had answered an advertisement for a used car when at least thirty whites carrying baseball bats, golf clubs, and at least one pistol attacked them. The whites reportedly thought that Hawkins and his friends had come into the area to visit a white girl. Police quickly arrested six white youths in connection with the attack.

Following the Bensonhurst incident, the clergyman Al Sharpton and other local civil rights activists led two days of angry demonstrations through the largely Italian-American neighborhood. It was the largest and most bitter disturbance in New York since December, 1986, when a black man was killed while fleeing a white mob in the Howard Beach section of Queens. (Also see entries dated August 30, 1989; August 31, 1989; May 18, 1990; and June 11, 1990.)

August 26. In Washington, D.C., about 30,000 men, women, and children staged a reenactment of the NAACP's famous "Silent March" of 1917.

The 1917 march down Fifth Avenue in New York City had been held to protest lynching and racial segregation. (See entry dated July 28, 1917.) The 1989 march was intended to persuade the U.S. Congress to reverse several recent decisions of the U.S. Supreme Court. Civil rights groups and others believed that these decisions had weakened affirmative action laws and minority "set aside" programs. Many of the demonstrators wore signs reading, "What the court has torn asunder, let Congress set right."

August 28. In Vineland, New Jersey, 200 blacks rioted a day after police killed Samuel Williams, a twenty-six-year-old black man. Officers had been in the process of arresting Williams on drug and weapon charges when he allegedly attacked them with a rod. No drugs or weapons were found on his body, however.

The disturbances left forty businesses and twenty cars damaged. Twenty-three people were arrested in the city of 54,000, located forty miles southeast of Philadelphia, Pennsylvania.

WILDERMUTH

August 30. More than 300 mourners attended funeral services for Yusef Hawkins, an African American youth shot to death in the predominately white section of Bensonhurst in Brooklyn, New York. (See entry dated August 23, 1989.) Another 1,000 persons who could not enter the church stood outside singing and listening to the eulogies.

Among those who were at the ceremonies were New York City mayor Edward Koch, New York governor Mario Cuomo, Republican mayoral candidate Rudolph Giuliani, African American mayoral candidate David Dinkins, and black film-maker Spike Lee. Mourners heckled Koch, Cuomo, and Giuliani outside the church, and Koch ended up leaving the ceremonies through a side door.

Al Sharpton, a civil rights activist who led protests immediately after the killing, said in one of the eulogies: "We're not going to let you down.... They're going to pay this time, Yusef. It's time for us to change our ways. We can run a man for the White House, but we can't walk a child through Bensonhurst."

Another speaker, minister Louis Farrakhan, a leader of the Nation of Islam, proclaimed: "We say, as the Jews say, Never again, Never again, Never again.... As long as white children can get away with killing black children, and white law enforcement does not know how to make examples of its own ... then justice is far off."

August 31. More than 7,000 people marched through the downtown section of Brooklyn, New York, as protests against the killing of sixteen-year-old Yusef Hawkins continued.

The march turned violent after reaching the Brooklyn Bridge, where police had set up barricades. The demonstrators charged through the barricades, setting off hand-to-hand battles between marchers and police. The rioters also threw bottles and rocks, and the police responded by using their nightsticks. At least 23 officers were injured; there were no immediate reports of injuries to civilians. (Also see entries dated August 23, 1989, and August 30, 1989.)

September 3. In Virginia Beach, Virginia, a confrontation between police and black college students on vacation left four people injured (two by gunfire) and led to the arrests of at least 160 people. Police said that more than 100 businesses were looted during the disturbance.

An estimated 10,000 people, mostly black students from eastern colleges and universities, had gone to the resort town for the Labor Day weekend. Some students who witnessed the riot said police "overreacted" to what was going on.

September 12. David Dinkins, the African American president of the Borough of Manhattan, defeated Mayor Edward Koch in the Democratic primary election for mayor of New York City. With this victory, he won the right to face Republican Rudolph Giuliani in the upcoming November elections.

September 16. *Forbes* magazine estimated that African American pop singer Michael Jackson would make $65 million in 1989 and would remain "the world's highest paid entertainer." The magazine placed his total earnings for 1988-89 at $125 million.

September 19. Gerald Turner, chancellor of the University of Mississippi, apologized to officials at predominantly black Rust College following a racial incident that involved members of the Beta Theta Pi fraternity at his university. He also ordered the fraternity's officers to apologize as well.

According to reports, members of the Beta Theta Pi fraternity dumped two naked white pledges (people who have promised to join the fraternity) on the Rust campus in Holly Springs, about 25 miles from the University of Mississippi campus at Oxford. On their chests were painted the slurs "KKK" and "We Hate Niggers." To escape from students who were chasing them, the naked pledges then ran into the Rust College security office.

The incident at Rust College was one of a series of similar occurrences aimed at black students on high school and college campuses across the nation throughout 1989.

September 20. A House of Representatives subcommittee voted unanimously to order former Housing and Urban Development (HUD) Secretary Samuel Pierce, Jr., to testify about alleged mismanagement at the department he headed during the administration of President Ronald Reagan.

Pierce had appeared voluntarily before the subcommittee back in May. Three times since then, however, he had asked for more time to prepare his testimony. Angry

275

congressmen felt he was just trying to avoid responsibility for his actions and decided to order him to appear on September 26.

The former HUD Secretary, who served from 1981 to 1989, was the only African American appointed to the cabinet of former president Reagan. (Also see entry dated December 22, 1980.)

September 20. The Armed Services Committee of the U.S. Senate voted unanimously to approve the nomination of General Colin Powell as chairman of the Joint Chiefs of Staff. The vote cleared the way for Powell to become the first African American ever to lead the joint military forces of the United States. (Also see entry dated August 10, 1989.)

October 3. Maynard Jackson was elected to a new term as mayor of Atlanta, Georgia. He scored a landslide victory over city councilman and veteran civil rights activist Hosea Williams to return to City Hall.

Jackson was first elected mayor of Atlanta in 1973, making him the first African American to be elected mayor of a major southern city since the Reconstruction era. He served two terms until 1982, when he became ineligible to run for a third consecutive term.

October 3. Forty-two-year-old Art Shell, former lineman for the Oakland Raiders of the National Football League (NFL) and a member of the Professional Football Hall of Fame, was named head coach of the Los Angeles Raiders. The appointment made Shell the first black head coach in the NFL since Fritz Pollard was a player-coach for the Hammond (Indiana) Pros from 1923 until 1925.

October 6. Two former employees of Shoney's restaurants, one black, one white, filed a federal lawsuit in Georgia claiming that the restaurant chain practiced racial discrimination.

The black plaintiff, Jackie Montgomery, said she was forbidden to work in a Shoney's dining room because company policy maintained that "blacks should not be allowed out front," especially in restaurants located in predominantly white neighborhoods. The white plaintiff, Cylinda Adams, said that she complained to several supervisors about the alleged racism and was fired because of it.

The Atlanta suit was filed only four months after a similar charge was brought before the courts in Florida. And it was only two months after Shoney's executives signed an affirmative action agreement with the Southern Christian Leadership Conference (SCLC). In that agreement, Shoney's promised to provide $90 million in jobs and minority business participation over the next three years. Included were pledges to recruit and train blacks for managerial positions and to give scholarships to African American students interested in the food service industry. (Also see entry dated November, 1992.)

October 11. J. Rupert Picott, educator and lobbyist, died of cancer in Washington, D.C., at the age of sixty-nine.

Picott, a native of Suffolk, Virginia, received his undergraduate degree at Virginia Union University in Richmond, a master's degree in education from Temple University in Philadelphia, Pennsylvania, and a doctorate degree in education from Harvard University. During the 1940s, he became executive secretary of the black Virginia Teachers Association. After the 1954 decision of the U.S. Supreme Court in *Brown v. Board of Education,* some school systems in Virginia tried to fire some of their black teachers. Picott then took action to protect their jobs.

From 1969 until 1985, Picott was best known as executive director of the Association for the Study of Afro-American Life and History (ASALH). In this position, he worked to promote the study and celebration of African American history. Perhaps his greatest accomplishment was convincing both state and federal governments to proclaim February as Black History Month.

October 11. The principal and a student of Minor High School in Adamsville, Alabama, were stabbed during a fight between black and white students.

Tensions had increased in the days just before the incident, and several fights had broken out between blacks and whites. In an effort to bring peace, principal Judson Jones tried to arrange a meeting of black and white students. Before the meeting could get started, a fight erupted, and Jones was stabbed.

These racial disturbances in Alabama were a part of the growing number of such encounters on high school and college campuses throughout the year.

October 12. Describing themselves as "shocked and appalled," several of the nation's most prominent civil rights leaders sent a telegram to the clergyman Ralph

Abernathy, former head of the Southern Christian Leadership Conference (SCLC). In the telegram, they urged him to reject his claims that the late Dr. Martin Luther King, Jr., had spent part of the last night of his life with two different women.

Abernathy had made the accusations in his recently released autobiography, *And the Walls Came Tumbling Down*. Many of the book's opponents questioned its accuracy and charged Abernathy with being irresponsible.

In his response, Abernathy explained: "In including some of the things in the book, I have had to agonize, balancing my need to tell a complete and honest story with what I know to be my responsibility to respect the privacy and dignity of the living and the dead.... I can only say that I have written nothing in malice and omitted nothing out of cowardice." (Also see entry dated October 24, 1989.)

October 18. The White House revealed that President George Bush had accepted the resignation of William Barclay Allen as chairman of the U.S. Commission on Civil Rights (CCR).

During his time in office, Allen had been at the center of numerous controversies that led many people to criticize his leadership. The most recent uproar was caused by a speech he had given entitled, "Blacks? Animals? Homosexuals? What Is a Minority?" (Also see entry dated February 23, 1990.)

October 20. Alcee Hastings, a black U.S. District Court judge from Florida, was convicted by the U.S. Senate on charges relating to conspiracy and perjury. He became only the sixth federal official in American history to be removed from office by impeachment (when a public official is found guilty of misconduct in his or her job).

After the verdict, Hastings remarked, "I don't accept this as a reading of Al Hastings the man. I didn't commit a crime.... There may be something about me—my outspokenness and what have you—that allows that maybe it's best that I'm out of this particular arena." He announced that he would later seek the Democratic nomination for governor of Florida. (Also see entries dated March 16, 1989, and November 3, 1992.)

October 24. Two civil rights activists, Abjua Abi Naantaanbuu and Bernard Lee, disputed claims about Martin Luther King, Jr., that Ralph Abernathy made in his autobiography, *And the Walls Came Tumbling Down*.

Naantaanbuu and Lee, both of whom were with the civil rights leader the night before his assassination, accused Abernathy of being drunk and asleep at the time he says he knew King had affairs with two different women. Abernathy had implied in his book that one of those women was Naantaanbuu. She later sued Abernathy for "falsely and maliciously" leading people to believe that she had been intimate with King on the last night of his life. (Also see entry dated October 12, 1989.)

November 5. Thousands attended the dedication of a monument to martyrs of the civil rights movement in downtown Montgomery, Alabama.

Designed by architect/sculptor Maya Lin for the Southern Poverty Law Center, the memorial consists of a long, curved wall of black granite over which flows a thin sheet of water. In front of the wall is a twelve-foot in diameter disk that seems to "float" above the plaza below; a thin sheet of water flows over it, too. Inscribed on the disk are the names of more than forty civil rights activists who died during the struggle, including Martin Luther King, Jr.

November 7. David Dinkins, the president of the Borough of Manhattan, was elected mayor of New York City, becoming the first African American ever to occupy that office. Dinkins, a sixty-two-year-old Democrat, won a narrow victory over Republican challenger Rudolph Giuliani.

In the race for mayor, Dinkins ran a moderate campaign designed to "soothe, not excite." He tried to appeal to the city's ethnic diversity, which he called "a gorgeous mosaic." As a result, he was able to build a biracial coalition that carried him to victory. At the time of the election, only 25.2 percent of New York City's eight million people were black.

November 7. Virginia's lieutenant-governor, L. Douglas Wilder, achieved a narrow victory over his Republican rival, J. Marshall Coleman, to become the first black elected governor in American history. The only other black to occupy a governor's office was P.B.S. Pinchback, who served as acting governor of Louisiana for a month at the end of 1872. (See entry dated December 11, 1872.)

Wilder, the grandson of slaves, was born in Richmond, Virginia, in 1931. He received a bachelor's degree in chemistry from Virginia Union University in 1951 and a law degree from the Howard University School of Law in 1959. Wilder then returned to Richmond to open his own practice and soon developed a reputation as a successful and somewhat flamboyant trial attorney.

Wilder's political career began in 1970, when he was elected to the Virginia State Senate. Although he had not been active in the civil rights movement of the 1960s, he immediately made a name for himself in the senate with "a blistering attack" on the state song, "Carry Me Back to Old Virginny." He and other blacks objected to "the sentimental [melody] about a slave pining for the plantation." While the song was not officially dropped, it was played much less often at public gatherings.

While a member of the senate, Wilder also led a campaign to make the birthday of Martin Luther King, Jr., a state holiday. The best he could do, however, was to have King's name added to a holiday for Confederate generals Robert E. Lee and Thomas "Stonewall" Jackson.

Wilder remained in the Virginia State Senate until 1986, when he became lieutenant-governor. At the time, he was the only black serving in that position in the country.

November 10. The Rhythm and Blues Foundation presented its first career achievement awards at the Smithsonian Institution in Washington, D.C.

The idea for the awards came from Howell Begle, a Washington attorney who has been a life-long soul music fan and admirer of blues singer Ruth Brown. After Begle discovered that Brown and dozens of other rhythm and blues artists had experienced financial difficulties in the mid-1960s, he established the Rhythm and Blues Foundation to help them. He later named blind blues singer Ray Charles chairman of the organization. The group eventually raised $1.5 million, donated mostly by Atlantic Records Company.

Several of the honorees performed for the audience. Among them were Percy Sledge, whose "When a Man Loves a Woman" was the first soul recording to rise to the top of the pop music charts; Mary Wells, famous for her recordings of "My Guy" and "You Beat Me to the Punch"; Charles Brown, who sang "Driftin' Blues" and "Black Night"; and Ruth Brown, often called "Miss Rhythm."

Each winner of the Rhythm and Blues award received a check for $15,000 in order to right "some past wrongs" as well as recognize lifetime achievement.

November 30. About 200 people gathered to protest racism at the Tuscaloosa campus of the University of Alabama and the school's financial investments in the Republic of South Africa.

The protest was sparked by an incident that took place during a football game on October 14th. At that game, some spectators jeered Kimberly Ashely, the university's black homecoming queen. The protestors also objected to the prominent display of Confederate flags.

December 1. Alvin Ailey, African American dancer and choreographer, died of a blood disorder in New York City at the age of fifty-eight.

Ailey was born in the rural town of Rogers, Texas, where he faced discrimination at a very early age. An outstanding high school athlete, he then went on to study dance while he briefly attended college. He founded the Alvin Ailey American Dance Theater in 1958 and began giving concerts regularly. The group made a successful tour of Australia in 1962 and was a major hit in Europe in 1965.

Although Ailey retired from performing twenty years before his death, he continued to compose and arrange many of his troupe's dances, including seventy-nine ballets. In the words of one critic, he created "a choreographic style distinctly his own—a combination of modern, ballet, jazz, and ethnic [dance]."

Perhaps Ailey's best-known work was "Revelations," a piece dating back to 1961 that was based on his childhood experiences in black Baptist churches. He also liked to honor the works of other people he admired or with whose causes he sympathized. For example, he choreographed "For Bird with Love" as a tribute to jazz saxophonist Charlie "Bird" Parker, whose career was shortened by drug abuse. In collaboration with jazz drummer Max Roach, Ailey choreographed a piece called "Survivors" to honor South African antiapartheid activists Nelson and Winnie Mandela.

In recognition of his many achievements, Ailey received New York's Handel Medallion and the Samuel H. Scripps American Dance Festival Award for lifetime contributions to modern dance. In 1988, he was honored at the Kennedy Center in Washington, D.C., for lifetime achievement in the performing arts. According to Professor Richard Long, author of *The Black Tradition in American Dance,* Ailey was simply "the best-known American dancer in the world."

December 6. Nathan I. Huggins, a leading scholar of African American culture, died of cancer in Boston, Massachusetts at the age of sixty-two.

Huggins was the author of works on the black antislavery leader Frederick Douglass and on the Harlem Renaissance, the black cultural movement of the 1920s. Since 1980, he had been professor of history and Afro-American Studies and director of the W.E.B. Du Bois Institute for Afro-American Research at Harvard University.

December 7. Percy Snow, African American linebacker for the Michigan State University Spartans, was awarded the Vince Lombardi trophy in Houston, Texas. The Lombardi trophy, named for the legendary coach of the Green Bay Packers, is awarded every year to the nation's top collegiate lineman.

On December 5, Snow had also won a Dick Butkus Award for his outstanding feats as a linebacker. At the time, he held the Michigan State record of 164 tackles.

December 11. A state appeals court in New York reversed the convictions of three white men who had been found guilty in the 1986 death of Michael Griffith, a black man, in the Howard Beach section of Queens, New York.

The unanimous ruling found that the trial judge had made two errors in his instructions to the jury. The three defendants—William Bollander, Thomas Farino, and James Povinelli, all aged nineteen—had been convicted in 1988 of second-degree riot charges for their part in the 1986 racial attack. (Also see entries dated December 20-23, 1986; January 23, 1988; and February 11, 1988.)

December 16-20. In four different cities in the South, two mail bombs killed a federal judge and a civil rights attorney, and authorities found and defused two other mail bombs before they exploded.

On December 16, a mail bomb exploded in the home of Robert S. Vance, a judge on the U.S. Court of Appeals for the Eleventh Circuit, in Birmingham, Alabama. Over the past ten years, the Eleventh Circuit had handled many civil rights cases, including ones involving school desegregation. Two days later, a mail bomb exploded in the office of Robert E. Robinson, an attorney in Savannah, Georgia, who had represented the NAACP and other clients in civil rights cases. Both men died instantly.

On December 19, law enforcement officials found and defused a mail bomb at the U.S. Court of Appeals for the Eleventh Circuit in Atlanta, Georgia. The Appeals Court had handled many of the South's civil rights suits over the past decade. That same day, a mail bomb found outside the headquarters of the Jacksonville, Florida, chapter of the NAACP did not explode.

Shortly after the incidents, the FBI announced that all four of the packages had been mailed from Georgia. The FBI also said it suspected the same person (or persons) was behind the killings and that he (or they) were probably "white supremacists." (Also see entry dated August 21, 1989.)

December 24. Ernest "Dutch" Morial, the first black mayor of New Orleans, Louisiana, died of an apparent heart attack in New Orleans at the age of sixty.

Morial was born in New Orleans on October 9, 1929. In 1954, he became the first black law school graduate of Louisiana State University. His public service career began in 1960 when he was elected president of the NAACP chapter in New Orleans. Working with fellow civil rights activist A.P. Tureard, he filed lawsuits against the city over segregation in public facilities and institutions.

In 1965, Morial became the first black assistant U.S. Attorney in Louisiana. Two years later, he became the first black legislator since the Reconstruction era. He served as a member of the State House of Representatives from 1967 to 1970, then became the first black ever elected to Louisiana's 4th Circuit Court of Appeals in 1973.

In 1977, on the strength of a huge black vote, Morial became the first black mayor of New Orleans. As mayor for two terms (a total of eight years), he had to deal with destructive floods in 1978, a police strike that crippled the city's annual Mardi Gras festival in 1979, and a financially troubled world exposition in 1984. Morial left office in 1986 following an unsuccessful attempt to change the city charter to allow the mayor to serve a third four-year term.

On the national scene, Morial had served as president of the National Conference of Mayors, a member of the Democratic National Committee (DNC), and one of the key black advisors to the Democratic presidential candidate Michael Dukakis in 1988.

1990   **January 10.** Forty-six-year-old Marcelite J. Harris became the first African American woman to be named brigadier general in the U.S. Air Force.

Born in Houston, Texas, in 1943, Harris earned a bachelor's degree in speech and drama from Spelman College in 1964. She then earned a second bachelor's degree in business management from the University of Maryland.

Harris entered the Air Force in 1965 and served in California, Germany, and Illinois, where she became the Air Force's first female aircraft maintenance officer. She then served in Thailand and again in California before being named personnel staff officer at Air Force Headquarters in Washington, D.C., in 1975. During that assignment, she also served as a White House aide to President Jimmy Carter.

In 1978, Harris left Washington for the U.S. Air Force Academy in Colorado, where she led a cadet squadron for two years. Since then, she has returned to the field of aircraft maintenance, serving in various command positions on Air Force bases in Kansas, Japan, Mississippi, and Oklahoma.

February 4-7. Four black protesters were arrested after a disturbance in the mayor's office in Selma, Alabama, on February 4. They were protesting the earlier dismissal of Norward Roussell as the first black superintendent of the city's schools. The Selma Board of Education had said that Roussell's "managerial skills" were not good enough.

The trouble dated back to December, 1989, when six white members of the Selma Board of Education voted against extending Superintendent Roussell's contract. The five black members of the board then resigned in protest, and black students boycotted several of the city's schools.

On February 6, the Selma Board of Education offered to rehire Superintendent Roussell on a temporary basis and asked the five black members of the board to return to their posts. The next day, hundreds of demonstrators protested at City Hall. They demanded that Roussell be permanently rehired. They also claimed that police had roughed up one of the women arrested during the February 4 protest. Meanwhile, the city's schools, which were 70 percent black, remained closed.

February 11. On orders from the new president of South Africa, Frederick W. de Klerk, human rights activist Nelson Mandela was released from prison after serving nearly thirty years. The sixty-two-year-old Mandela had long been the major symbol of the struggle against apartheid (racial segregation) in his country, and political and human rights leaders around the world greeted the news of his release with applause.

In 1986, the U.S. Congress had passed an Anti-Apartheid Act that restricted the kinds of economic activity between the United States and the white minority government of South Africa. (The Congress overrode President Ronald Reagan's veto to pass the act. He had claimed it was too harsh.) The act said that the United States would lift these sanctions, or economic restrictions, only after South Africa had met several requirements. Among those requirements were freeing Mandela and legalizing his antiapartheid group, the African National Congress (ANC).

On February 2, 1990, President de Klerk finally ended a thirty-year-old ban on the ANC. A little more than a week later came Mandela's release.

Randall Robinson, executive director of Trans-Africa, the leading antiapartheid group in the United States, expressed the great delight most African Americans felt upon hearing that Mandela was free. But he warned that the sanctions must remain in place and that "it would be a mistake ... at this juncture for President Bush to invite President de Klerk to visit the U.S." (Also see entry dated June 20-30, 1990.)

February 11. James "Buster" Douglas, a twenty-four-year-old African American, knocked out Mike Tyson in the tenth round of a match in Tokyo, Japan, to take the world's heavyweight boxing championship in "a major upset."

February 21-24. Students at historically black Tennessee State University in Nashville staged sit-ins and marches protesting "poor conditions" at the school. Several students were arrested for "violating school rules or criminal laws" during the demonstrations.

February 23. President George Bush named African American businessman Arthur A. Fletcher to be chairman of the U.S. Commission on Civil Rights (CCR).

The sixty-five-year-old Fletcher had served with Bush when the president was U.S. Ambassador to the United Nations in 1971. Fletcher was an assistant secretary of labor in the administration of President Richard Nixon and deputy assistant for urban affairs for President Gerald Ford. In 1978, he lost the election for mayor of Washington, D.C., to Democrat Marion Barry.

Fletcher succeeded another black, William Barclay Allen. As chairman of the CCR, Allen had been involved in several controversies, even with fellow commissioners. (See entry dated October 18, 1989.) He and the man who served as chairman before him, the late Clarence Pendleton (who was also black), had made some civil rights leaders and members of Congress angry because they did not aggressively fight for civil rights enforcement. But the appointment of Fletcher drew praise because he was widely considered to be a fair-minded person.

March 3. Carole Gist, a twenty-year-old African American from Detroit, Michigan, was crowned "Miss USA" in Wichita, Kansas. Gist, a student at Northwood Institute, was the first black woman to win the beauty title. Three blacks had already won the older title of "Miss America." (Also see entry dated September 17, 1983.)

March 19. Harold Irwin Bearden, a minister and civic leader, died after suffering a stroke in Atlanta, Georgia, at the age of seventy-nine.

Bearden was born in Atlanta on May 8, 1910. He received his bachelor's degree at Morris Brown College and a divinity degree from Turner Theological Seminary. Bearden was ordained a deacon in the African Methodist Episcopal (AME) Church in 1930 and an elder in 1931. He pastored the Big Bethel AME Church, one of the oldest and largest congregations in Atlanta, from 1951 to 1964.

From 1960 to 1962, Bearden was an acting presiding elder of the AME Church. In 1964, he was consecrated a bishop in Cincinnati, Ohio. Bearden's first assignments as bishop were in Central and West Africa. While there, he was elected president of the board of trustees of Monrovia College in Liberia.

Upon his return to the United States, Bearden had church district assignments in Ohio and Texas before being named bishop of the Sixth Episcopal District in his native Georgia in 1976. He served in that position until 1980 and continued to serve on special assignments for his church until retiring in 1984.

While Bearden was president of the Atlanta chapter of the NAACP during the late 1950s, the group filed a lawsuit to desegregate the Atlanta public schools. Bearden was also one of several black ministers who were arrested in 1957 for defying Georgia's bus segregation laws. He always used his Sunday radio broadcasts to criticize both segregationists and black accommodationists about "Jim Crowism" in Atlanta and the nation. In addition, he supported student sit-in demonstrations in the city during the 1960s. In 1978, the state Senate of Georgia named him an outstanding citizen.

March 30. Thea Bowman, black Catholic educator, died of cancer in Jackson, Mississippi, at the age of fifty-two.

Bowman was the only African American member of the Franciscan Sisters of Perpetual Adoration. She served as director of intercultural awareness for its Jackson diocese and was a member of the faculty of the Institute of Black Catholic Studies at Xavier University in New Orleans, Louisiana.

She was widely honored for her educational work as well as her pioneering efforts to encourage black Catholics "to express their cultural roots inside the church." In 1989, she received the U.S. Catholic Award from *U.S. Catholic Magazine* "for furthering the cause of women in the Roman Catholic Church." In addition, the Sister Thea Bowman Black Catholic Educational Foundation was established in 1989 "to provide financial support for black students in Catholic primary and elementary schools and Catholic colleges and universities."

In 1988, Bowman recorded an album, *Sister Thea: Songs of My People*, which consisted of fifteen black spirituals. The recording made the nun a popular figure at conventions and on college campuses across the nation.

April 4. Sarah Vaughan, African American jazz singer known affectionately as "the Divine One," died of cancer in California at the age of sixty-six.

Vaughan was born on March 27, 1924, in Newark, New Jersey. She joined a Baptist church choir as a child, and the gospel influence remained with her throughout her career. (She occasionally included a version of "The Lord's Prayer" in her performances.) Vaughan's mother wanted her daughter to pursue a career in classical music, so she sent young Sarah to weekly organ and piano lessons. But Vaughan soon headed down a different path. At age eighteen, she won a talent contest at Harlem's Apollo Theatre with her version of "Body and Soul." She was soon singing and playing piano with the Earl Hines Band and later toured with Billy Eckstine.

Vaughan began a solo career in the 1940s. From then until her death, she performed before jazz audiences throughout the nation and recorded at least three Top 10 pop singles, including "Broken-Hearted Melody," which sold more than a million records. Among her other notable recordings were "Misty" and the albums *The Divine Sarah Vaughan, Gershwin Live*, and *Lover Man*. At the 1989 Grammy Award ceremonies, Vaughan received a special Lifetime Achievement Award.

April 17. Ralph Abernathy, minister and civil rights leader, died of heart problems in Atlanta, Georgia, at the age of sixty-four.

Abernathy was born on March 11, 1926, in Linden, Alabama. After his discharge from the U.S. Army in 1945, he enrolled in Alabama State College in Montgomery and earned his bachelor's degree in 1950. It was while he was attending graduate school at Atlanta University that Abernathy first met Martin Luther King, Jr.

Before becoming involved in the civil rights movement, Abernathy was a dean at Alabama State College and a part-time pastor of a church in Demopolis, Alabama. In 1948, he was named pastor of the black First Baptist Church in Montgomery, Alabama.

When Martin Luther King, Jr., arrived in Montgomery in 1954 to become pastor of the Dexter Avenue Baptist Church, he received a warm welcome from Abernathy and their friendship grew stronger. King had planned to spend two or three years getting himself established in the city before becoming active in civic affairs. Abernathy, on the other hand, wanted to return to his graduate studies. In 1955, however, their plans were disrupted by the arrest of Rosa Parks and the Montgomery bus boycott that followed. Both men served as leaders during the protest— King as the major spokesman and Abernathy as his top assistant.

For the next thirteen years, Abernathy remained King's closest helper, friend, and supporter. Together they participated in the civil rights struggles of Montgomery, Albany, Birmingham, Selma, Chicago, Memphis, and dozens of other cities and towns.

After an assassin's bullet struck down King in Memphis, Tennessee, on April 4, 1968, it was Abernathy who cradled his fallen comrade in his arms and remained with him through his death and the autopsy that followed. He gave one of the principal eulogies at King's funeral, held on what he called "one of the darkest days in American history." As the slain civil rights leader had wished, Abernathy then took King's place as president of the Southern Christian Leadership Conference (SCLC).

Shortly after King's death, Abernathy led the "Poor People's Campaign" for jobs and freedom in Washington, D.C. (See entry dated May 11, 1968.) He remained active in the civil rights movement until resigning from the SCLC in 1977.

Abernathy then turned to politics. He ran unsuccessfully for Congress in a race to fill the seat vacated by Andrew Young when he became ambassador to the United

Nations. In 1980, Abernathy was one of the few national black leaders to endorse the Republican presidential candidate Ronald Reagan over President Jimmy Carter. And in 1984, he broke with some of his old colleagues in the civil rights movement and endorsed Jesse Jackson for president of the United States.

In the months just before his death, Abernathy became the target of considerable criticism from many civil rights leaders for accusing Martin Luther King, Jr., of spending part of the last night of his life with two different women. The accusations were contained in Abernathy's autobiography, *And the Walls Came Tumbling Down.* (See entries dated October 12, 1989, and October 24, 1989.)

April 27. A federal court jury in Memphis, Tennessee, announced that it was unable to reach a verdict in the case of Harold Ford, a black U.S. representative.

Ford, a Tennessee Democrat, had been charged with bank fraud, mail fraud, and conspiracy. He was specifically accused of taking more than $1 million in "political payoffs disguised as loans" from bankers C.H. and Jake Butcher of Knoxville, Tennessee. Ford had consistently maintained his innocence and suggested that the charges against him were racially motivated. (Also see entry dated April 9, 1993.)

May 13. In a colorful ceremony at which African dancers and gospel singers performed, George Augustus Stallings was ordained the first bishop of the African-American Catholic Church.

The forty-one-year-old black priest had broken away from the Roman Catholic Church in June, 1989, after declaring that it had failed to meet the needs of its African American parishioners. On July 4, 1989, Church officials suspended him for "founding an independent black congregation."

At the time Stallings became a bishop, his African-American Catholic Church had expanded from Washington, D.C., to the cities of Baltimore, Maryland; Norfolk, Virginia; and Philadelphia, Pennsylvania.

May 16. Sammy Davis, Jr., versatile African American entertainer and America's "Ambassador of Goodwill," died of cancer in Beverly Hills, California, at the age of sixty-four.

Born on December 8, 1925, in the Harlem section of New York City, Davis began performing in vaudeville at the age of three with the Will Mastin Trio. (The other two members were his father, Sam, Sr., and a man he called his "uncle," Will Mastin.) He continued to tour with the Trio throughout the 1930s and made his movie debut in 1933 appearing with Ethel Waters in *Rufus Jones for President.*

Davis left the Trio to serve in the Army during World War II but entertained the troops as a writer, director, and producer of camp shows. After the war, he rejoined his father and uncle and began his steady climb to superstardom.

Davis's talents as a dancer, singer, and actor were greatly respected on the stage and in nightclubs as well as in film and television. He often worked with his longtime friends Frank Sinatra and Dean Martin.

Among Davis's most popular recordings were "The Way You Look Tonight" (1946), "Hey There" (1954), "That Old Black Magic" (1955), "The Shelter of Your Arms" (1964), "I've Got to Be Me" (1969), and "The Candy Man" (1972). He made his Broadway debut in 1956 in the musical *Mr. Wonderful* and won a Tony nomination for his starring role as a boxer in *Golden Boy.*

On film, Davis had major roles in *Anna Lucasta* (1958), *Porgy and Bess* (1959), *Oceans Eleven* (1960), *Robin and the Seven Hoods* (1964), and *Sweet Charity* (1969). His last film appearance was in 1989 with dancer Gregory Hines in *Tap.* Between 1956 and 1980, Davis also appeared on almost every variety show and comedy series on network television. In 1966, he starred in his own television series, one of the first ever hosted by a black person.

Davis supported the civil rights movement of the 1960s by singing at fundraisers, especially for Dr. Martin Luther King, Jr. (Davis was with King at the end of the famous Selma to Montgomery voting rights march in Alabama in 1965.) He also helped to raise money for the defense of black activist Angela Davis.

Davis was also a frequent target of controversy. In 1961, for example, his invitation to an inaugural event for President John F. Kennedy was withdrawn out of fear that his presence there with the woman who was then his wife, Swedish actress Mai Britt, would "inflame Southerners." Davis also made headlines in 1972 at a function for President Richard Nixon during the Republican National Convention. He startled the President and especially many African Americans when he came up behind Nixon and gave him a big hug while flashing a wide grin.

The rise of Davis from demeaning, stereotypical roles in vaudeville and his early films to the highest rank of American entertainment is documented in his autobiographies, *Yes, I Can* (1965) and *Why Me?* (1989). At the time of his death, Davis had become, in the words of NAACP executive director Benjamin Hooks, "an American treasure that the whole world loved."

May 18. Nineteen-year-old Joseph Fama was convicted of second degree murder in the August 23, 1989, slaying of Yusuf Hawkins, a sixteen-year-old black youth, in the Bensonhurst section of New York City.

The mob attack that led to Hawkins's death in an all-white neighborhood had been the focus of racial tension in the nation's largest city for more than six months. Some blacks also pointed to the incident as evidence of increasing racism in the United States. (Also see entries dated August 23, 1989; August 30, 1989; August 31, 1989; and June 11, 1990.)

June 3. Bobby Rush, former leader of the militant Black Panther Party in Chicago, became deputy chairman of the Illinois Democratic Party. A Chicago alderman since 1983, Rush had quietly gained political clout in the city where he once declared that "the power structure has genocide in their minds" and that the solution was revolution.

Rush had first run for alderman in 1974 shortly after leaving the Panthers. He lost that election but tried again in 1983 and was helped into office by the popularity of Harold Washington, Chicago's first black mayor. (Also see entry dated November 3, 1992.)

June 6. Harvey Gantt, the first African American mayor of Charlotte, North Carolina, won his state's Democratic nomination for the U.S. Senate. The forty-seven-year-old architect was the first black person in the history of the state of North Carolina to receive the Democratic Party's nomination for U.S. senator.

As the Democrat nominee, Gantt would have to face the veteran Republican senator Jesse Helms in the November, 1990, general elections.

June 11. In New York City, two nineteen-year-old white youths were sentenced to prison for the 1989 shooting death of Yusuf Hawkins, a sixteen-year-old black youth.

Joseph Fama, who prosecutors and police authorities said actually shot Hawkins, was sentenced to thirty-two-and-two-thirds years to life in prison. His friend Keith

Mondello received a sentence of five-and-one-third to sixteen years in prison and a $2,000 fine. He had been identified as the ringleader of the mob that attacked Hawkins and three other blacks in the Bensonhurst neighborhood of New York City in 1989. (Also see entries dated August 23, 1989; August 30, 1989; August 31, 1989; and May 18, 1990.)

June 13. Marion Barry, mayor of Washington, D.C., announced that he would not seek a fourth term.

At the time of the announcement, Barry was on trial in a federal district court in Washington. He had been arrested on January 18, 1990, in a "drug sting" at a local hotel. The mayor had pleaded innocent to lying to a grand jury about his alleged drug use, several cocaine possession charges, and a cocaine conspiracy charge. (Also see entries dated October 11, 1991; April, 1992; and September, 1992.)

June 20-30. Nelson Mandela, deputy president of the African National Congress (ANC) and the major symbol of the struggle for freedom in the Republic of South Africa, conducted a major tour of the United States. The ten-day visit was designed to convince Americans to maintain economic sanctions against the white-minority government in South Africa until it ended its system of racial apartheid. Mandela also hoped to raise money to help the ANC's campaign for majority rule.

On June 20, Mandela was honored with a ticker-tape parade in downtown New York City, where approximately 750,000 people lined the streets to greet him. Two days later, the South African freedom fighter spoke at the United Nations (UN). During the many years Mandela was in prison, the UN had regularly adopted resolutions opposing South African apartheid. The speeches delegates and others gave condemning the system usually ended with the words, "Free Mandela."

After leaving New York City, Mandela moved on to Boston, Massachusetts, and Washington, D.C., where he met with President George Bush on June 26. Before leaving the capital, Mandela also spoke to a joint session of the U.S. Congress. He recalled the names of Frederick Douglass, Thomas Jefferson, Joe Louis, and other American heroes and repeated his plea for a continuation of sanctions against the white-minority government in South Africa. Members of Congress greeted his remarks with several thunderous standing ovations.

On June 27, Mandela visited Atlanta, Georgia, the city that is known as the capital of the civil rights movement. There he placed a wreath at the tomb of slain civil rights leader Martin Luther King, Jr., and spoke at a rally of more than 50,000 people.

"We are ... conscious that here in the southern part of the country, you have experienced the degradation of racial segregation," Mandela told the mostly black crowd. "We continue to be inspired by the knowledge that in the face of your own difficulties, you are in the forefront of the antiapartheid movement in this country." Then, drawing on King's famous "I Have a Dream" speech, Mandela declared, "Let freedom ring, let us all acclaim now, 'Let freedom ring in South Africa. Let freedom ring wherever people's rights are trampled upon.'"

On June 28, Mandela made a brief visit to Miami Beach, Florida, where he spoke to the annual convention of the American Federation of State, County, and Municipal Employees (AFSCME). About 250 anti-Castro Cubans and Cuban-Americans protested his visit, however. They were angry because Mandela had expressed thanks for the Cuban dictator's support of the antiapartheid movement and also because he had refused to condemn Castro during an appearance on the "Nightline" television program.

Mandela then moved on to Detroit, Michigan, where he addressed a rally of 50,000 people. There he met Rosa Parks, the Alabama seamstress who had sparked the famous Montgomery bus boycott. Later that same evening, Mandela and his group were honored at a rally held at Tiger Stadium.

On June 29 and 30, Mandela ended his American tour in California with stops in Los Angeles and Oakland. He spoke to a crowd of 80,000 people at the Los Angeles Memorial Coliseum, declaring that "our masses in action are like a raging torrent. We are on freedom road, and nothing is going to stop us from reaching our destination."

Some Americans expressed serious concerns about Mandela's views, especially his refusal to condemn Cuban dictator Fidel Castro, Libya's "pro-terrorist" leader Muammar al-Qaddafi, and Palestine Liberation Organization (PLO) chief Yassar Arafat. Mandela's unwillingness to abandon the use of violence in his struggle also disturbed some people. Yet by and large, the South African leader was very warmly received by most Americans during his tour.

June 25. Mollie Lewis Moon, the founder of the National Urban League Guild (NULG), died from an apparent heart attack in Long Island City, New York, at the age of eighty-two.

Moon founded the NULG in 1942 to raise money for various Urban League programs. Under her leadership, the guild grew to eighty units, with 30,000 volunteers in the United States.

A major guild event was the annual Beaux Arts Ball, which Moon directed over for nearly fifty years. It began at the old Savoy Ballroom in the Harlem section of New York City in 1942 but moved downtown in 1948. In that particular year, Winthrop Rockefeller, a New York financier and philanthropist, arranged for the ball to be held in the Rainbow Room at the top of Rockefeller Center. Moon later recalled that the invitations to the event were sent out in both her name and that of Rockefeller. "Nobody was going to buck the landlord," she explained. "That's how we broke the color barrier."

July. In Atlanta, Georgia, Eugene Marino, the first black archbishop in the United States, resigned from his post after church authorities learned he had been having an affair with a young woman named Vicki Long. Long later claimed that she and Marino had been married since December, 1988, and that he was the father of her daughter. (Also see entry dated March 15, 1988.)

August 17. Pearl Bailey, a legendary cabaret singer and actress known as the "Ambassador of Love," died of an apparent heart attack in Philadelphia, Pennsylvania, at the age of seventy-two.

Bailey was born on March 29, 1918, in Newport News, Virginia. She began her professional career in vaudeville, singing in small clubs in Pennsylvania and Washington, D.C. She then became a featured singer with several big bands, including Count Basie's. This led to engagements in New York City in 1941. After touring with the USO during World War II, Bailey made her first appearance on a New York stage in a play called *St. Louis Woman*.

Throughout the rest of her career, Bailey kept busy making records, singing in nightclubs, and appearing on stage, in the movies, and on television. Her success came partly because she used her talent to rise above the racial stereotypes that hindered many other black performers of her time. Audiences everywhere responded enthusiastically to her easy-going style and mischievous wit. As she once told an interviewer, "If I just sang a song, it would mean nothing." Her greatest triumph came in 1967 when she starred with Cab Calloway in the all-black version of the Broadway hit *Hello, Dolly*.

During the 1970s, Bailey turned her attention to other activities. While she continued to perform occasionally, she also pursued her interest in international relations as a special advisor to the U.S. Mission to the United Nations. And in 1978, she enrolled in Georgetown University with the goal of becoming a teacher.

September 11. In Washington, D.C., Sharon Pratt Dixon, Eleanor Holmes Norton, and Jesse Jackson were victorious at the polls. All were newcomers to local politics.

Dixon won the Democratic mayoral nomination after promising voters that she would clean up the district government following the scandals that rocked Mayor Marion Barry's administration. Norton won her bid to the House of Representatives, where she replaced longtime congressman Walter Fauntroy. And Jackson was elected "statehood senator"—a new office created by the Washington city council to help lobby Congress for district statehood.

October 16. Art Blakey, drummer and jazz band leader, died in New York City. He was seventy-one.

Blakey was a powerful and influential jazz talent who had a lifelong knack for identifying and nurturing gifted musicians. In 1954, along with Horace Silver, he founded the constantly changing band known as the Jazz Messengers. The group served as a virtual school for up-and-coming musicians, including Freddie Hubbard, Wayne Shorter, Branford and Wynton Marsalis, Donald Byrd, and McCoy Tyner. Among the older "graduates" of the Jazz Messengers are such notable musicians as Keith Jarrett, Chuck Mangione, Chick Corea, Terence Blanchard, Jackie McLean, and Donald Harrison.

October 22. President George Bush vetoed the Civil Rights Bill of 1990, saying the document "employs a maze of highly legalistic language to introduce the destructive force of quotas" in the workplace. Two days later, an attempt to override the veto in the Senate fell one vote short of the necessary two-thirds majority. (Also see entry dated June 5, 1991.)

October. The Dade County, Florida, chapter of the National Bar Association (NBA), a group of primarily African American lawyers, called for a boycott against the city of Miami as a convention and meeting site for all business, professional, religious, labor and civic associations.

The organization was angry about the treatment Miami officials had given to South African antiapartheid leaders Nelson and Winnie Mandela during their visit earlier in the year. The Mandelas had not received an official welcome, and some local leaders had criticized Nelson Mandela for his praise of Fidel Castro, Yassar Arafat, and Muammar al-Qaddafi. (See entry dated June 20-30, 1990.)

The lawyers' group also condemned the widespread job discrimination in south Florida's hotel and tourism industry. NBA leaders charged that the industry was dominated by Hispanics who formed labor unions that shut blacks out of entry-level jobs in hotels and restaurants. (Also see entry dated May 12, 1993.)

November 6. Voters in the state of Arizona narrowly defeated a special proposal that would have given a paid holiday to state employees in honor of Martin Luther King, Jr. At the time, only two other states, Montana and New Hampshire, did not observe a state holiday marking King's birthday.

The National Football League had threatened to move the 1993 Super Bowl XXVII from Phoenix unless the state adopted a King holiday. The defeat of the proposal also led to the cancellation of a golf tournament memorializing the slain civil rights leader as well as numerous other conventions and special events. (Also see entries dated January 18, 1988; January, 1992; and January 18, 1993.)

November 27. Charles Johnson, the author of *Middle Passage,* a novel about a freed slave and his adventures, won the 1990 National Book Award for fiction. He was the first African American male to win the award since Ralph Ellison won it in 1954 for *Invisible Man.*

1991 **January 29.** The Joint Center for Political and Economic Studies reported that most black Americans prefer to be called black, despite the growing use of the term African American.

Seventy-two percent of those polled preferred the designation black. Fifteen percent preferred African American, 3 percent preferred Afro-American, and 2 percent preferred Negro. (Also see entry dated December 28, 1988.)

January. "Brotherman," the comic superhero created by brothers David, Jason, and Guy Sims, became a hit with African American youths. The Simses created

Brotherman to provide a positive African American image for comic book readers. The first issue sold more than 8,000 copies.

February 9. James Cleveland, a Baptist clergyman and major figure in gospel music, died in Los Angeles, California, at the age of sixty.

Cleveland was a pianist, composer, arranger, promoter, and leader of the James Cleveland Singers. He also was the founder of the Gospel Music Workshop of America. During his career, Cleveland served as mentor, or guide, to Aretha Franklin, Billy Preston, and many other soul singers who got their starts in gospel music.

Cleveland wrote more than 400 gospel songs, including "Grace Is Sufficient," "Everything Will Be All Right," "He's Using Me," "The Man Jesus," "Peace Be Still," and "The Love of God." He recorded dozens of albums that sold millions of copies. Winner of three Grammy Awards, Cleveland was the first gospel singer to have a star on Hollywood's Walk of Fame.

February 26. The Detroit (Michigan) Board of Education approved an all-male academy for African American students. The approval came after intense debate over whether black boys should be segregated from black girls and white students.

Opponents argued that establishing such an academy creates the kind of school segregation that existed in the rural South before the landmark *Brown v. Board of Education* Supreme Court decision in 1954. (See entry dated May 17, 1954.) Others insisted that the academy and similar programs can help African Americans (especially young males) who need more support to overcome high dropout rates and the lack of positive male role models. (Also see entry dated June, 1991.)

March 3-5. In Los Angeles, California, black motorist Rodney King was severely beaten by several white police officers after being stopped for a speeding violation.

The beating was videotaped by George Holliday, who witnessed the incident from his nearby apartment balcony. The two-minute-long videotape revealed that the officers continued beating King with nightsticks even after they had put him in restraints and he appeared to be unable to fight back. Police officers on the scene said that King had led them on a high-speed chase and that he had resisted arrest.

The incident immediately caused an international uproar after the videotape appeared on network news programs. King spent two days in a hospital recovering from his injuries before being booked on charges of trying to escape from police officers. (Also see entries dated March 14, 1991; April 4-8, 1991; April 17, 1991; July 9, 1991; April 29-May 1, 1992; May 2, 1992; October 22, 1992; February 25, 1993; and April 17, 1993.)

March 7. James "Cool Papa" Bell, a Hall of Fame baseball player who once dazzled spectators with his base-running talents, died in St. Louis, Missouri, after a brief illness. He was eighty-seven years old.

Bell was sixteen years old when he began his career as a centerfielder who hit and threw left-handed. He played for the Homestead Grays, the St. Louis Stars, the Chicago American Giants, the Pittsburgh Crawfords, and the Kansas City Monarchs of the Negro Leagues. The schedule Bell followed was a rigorous one. For twenty-nine summers and twenty-one winters, he often played two and three games a day.

Although he once hit twenty-one home runs in a single season, Bell specialized in punching the ball and running. He was considered to be the fastest player in the old Negro Leagues. Most baseball historians believe that his $90 a month salary also made him the league's highest-paid player.

Bell batted .407 in 1946, his final season, but as a black man he could not play in the major leagues. His retirement came a year before Jackie Robinson broke the color barrier. Several major league teams later contacted Bell about playing again; one offered him an $8,000 contract. Realizing that his legs were no longer as good as they once had been, Bell rejected the offer so that he could preserve his image as the fastest man in the game.

After retiring from baseball, Bell went to work as a custodian at the St. Louis City Hall. He later was a night watchman.

March 14. A grand jury charged four Los Angeles, California, police officers— Stacey Koon, Theodore Briseno, Laurence Powell, and Timothy Wind— in the beating of black motorist Rodney King. The four were formally charged with one count of assault with a deadly weapon and one count of unnecessary assault or beating by a police officer. (Also see entries dated March 3-5, 1991; April 4-8, 1991; April 17, 1991; July 9, 1991; April 29-May 1, 1992; May 2, 1992; October 22, 1992; February 25, 1993 and April 17, 1993.)

March 25. The Academy of Motion Picture Arts and Science awarded comedienne and actress Whoopi Goldberg an Oscar for her supporting role in the movie *Ghost*. She was only the second African American female ever to win an Oscar. (See entry dated March, 1940.) Earlier, her performance in *Ghost* also earned her a Golden Globe Award and the Excellence Award at the Sixth Annual Women in Film Festival.

Goldberg was born Caryn Johnson in New York City's Chelsea section. Her other films include *The Color Purple, Jumpin' Jack Flash, Burglar, Fatal Beauty, Clara's Heart, The Long Walk Home, Soap Dish, Sister Act*, and *Made in America*. She received the NAACP's Image Award and an Academy Award nomination for her performance in *The Color Purple*. In 1990, the NAACP named her Black Entertainer of the Year.

April 4-8. Los Angeles Police Chief Darryl Gates was suspended with pay for sixty days by the Los Angeles Police Commission for "allegations of mismanagement and/or neglect of duty" in connection with the March 3 beating of motorist Rodney King.

On April 5, the City Council overturned the Police Commission's ruling, and Chief Gates returned to work on April 8. Mayor Tom Bradley had originally called for Gates's resignation. (Also see entries dated March 3-5, 1991; March 14, 1991; April 17, 1991; July 9, 1991; April 29-May 1, 1992; May 2, 1992; October 22, 1992; February 25, 1993 and April 17, 1993.)

April 28. Floyd McKissick, a lawyer and former national chairman of the Congress of Racial Equality (CORE), died in Durham, North Carolina. He was sixty-nine years old.

McKissick's long career as a civil rights activist was launched after he had trouble entering the all-white University of North Carolina Law School. He was finally admitted under a federal appeals court order after he enlisted the legal services of Thurgood Marshall, who was then an NAACP lawyer.

McKissick began practicing law in Durham, where he specialized in civil rights, criminal defense, and personal injury cases. He was national chairman of CORE from 1963 to 1966, when he succeeded James Farmer as director. (See entry dated January 3, 1966.) In 1990, McKissick served as a North Carolina District State judge.

May 26. Willy T. Ribbs became the first black to qualify and race in the Indianapolis 500. Engine problems forced him out in the sixth lap, however, and he finished in thirty-second place.

June 1. Fifty-year-old David Ruffin, a former lead singer with the Temptations, died of an apparent drug overdose in Philadelphia, Pennsylvania.

Born January 18, 1941, in Meridian, Mississippi, Ruffin joined the Temptations in the early 1960s. One of the group's three lead singers (the others were Eddie Kendrick and Paul Williams), he was the baritone voice behind the hits "My Girl," "Since I Lost My Baby," and "Ain't Too Proud to Beg." In 1969, Ruffin launched a solo career that lasted throughout most of the 1970s.

During the 1980s, Ruffin teamed up with Kendrick and another former Temptation, Dennis Edwards, on several projects. In 1985, for example, he and Kendrick recorded an album with Darryl Hall and John Oates. The album, "Live at the Apollo with David Ruffin and Eddie Kendrick," went gold. Later, they performed at the Live Aid benefit concert for African famine relief and then on the antiapartheid album *Sun City*. By the late 1980s, Ruffin, Kendrick, and Edwards were performing together regularly. In fact, Ruffin had returned to Philadelphia just three weeks before his death after a successful tour of England with his fellow Temptations.

June 5. Democrats in Congress tried to revive the vetoed Civil Rights Bill of 1990 (see entry dated October 22, 1990) by making changes to it that would help end discrimination against women. These changes would make it easier for workers to sue employers who do not hire a reasonable number of minorities and women.

June 23. White supremacist Tom Metzger, leader of the White Aryan Resistance, and three other men were ordered to stand trial for a 1983 cross-burning in a racially mixed suburb near Los Angeles, California. (Also see entry dated December 4, 1991.)

June 27. Citing his failing health and a demanding work schedule, eighty-three-year-old Justice Thurgood Marshall announced his retirement from the U.S. Supreme Court. He had served for twenty-four years as the Court's first and only black justice. In his remarks to reporters, Marshall condemned the conservative direction that the nation's highest court was taking. He declared that "power, not reason, is the new currency of this Court's decision-making."

A man of fierce pride, Marshall was well aware of his important role in American history. As a liberal member of the Court, he often influenced his fellow justices to keep in mind the less fortunate as they made their decisions. He earned a reputation for his outspoken interpretations of the first amendment to the Constitution and for his passionate attacks on discrimination.

According to J. Clay Smith, Jr., professor of constitutional law at the Howard University Law School, Thurgood Marshall "brought a diversity of viewpoints to the Court. [He] provided the Court the point of view of the poor in this country—black and white. I'm sure his experience and knowledge of poverty and segregation influenced the Justices, conservative and liberal alike." (Also see entries dated May 17, 1954; September 23, 1961; July 13, 1965; June 13, 1967; and January 24, 1993.)

June 30. In Memphis, Tennessee, the Lorraine Motel—where Martin Luther King, Jr., was assassinated in 1968—was converted into the National Civil Rights Museum. It was scheduled to open on July 4.

June. The Milwaukee (Wisconsin) public school system announced plans to open two experimental schools for 1,100 black male students. Officials hoped the experiment would encourage male students to stay in school and avoid a life of crime. (Also see entry dated February 26, 1991.)

July 1. President George Bush nominated forty-three-year-old Judge Clarence Thomas of the U.S. District of Columbia Court of Appeals to fill the Supreme Court vacancy created by the retirement of Thurgood Marshall. (See entry dated June 27, 1991).

Many African Americans were unhappy with the choice of Judge Thomas because he had strongly opposed affirmative action programs when he ran the Equal Employment Opportunity Commission (EEOC). (Thomas himself had attended the Yale University Law School under a program designed to admit minorities.) Yet some politicians and groups were reluctant to criticize an African American nominee, even though they really did not want to support a person who was as opposed to abortion or affirmative action as Thomas seemed to be. (Also see entries dated September 10-27, 1991, and October 6-15, 1991.)

July 9. In Los Angeles, California, an independent commission that was appointed following the Rodney King beating released a searing report condemning the Los Angeles Police Department (LAPD). The report stated that LAPD officers "are encouraged to command and confront, not to communicate." It also charged that racist and sexist behavior was widespread throughout the department.

The commission's panel offered many recommendations, including a "major overhaul" of the police department's procedures for disciplining officers and for handling citizens' complaints. The panel also advised replacing the Police Commission and suggested that Chief Darryl Gates retire as soon as a replacement could be hired. (Also see entries dated March 3-5, 1991; March 14, 1991; April 4-8, 1991; April 17, 1991; April 29-May 1, 1992; May 2, 1992; October 22, 1992; February 25, 1993 and April 17, 1993.)

July 12. Director John Singleton's movie *Boyz N the Hood* opened, featuring stars such as rap artist Ice Cube, Cuba Gooding, Jr., Larry Fishburne, and Morris Chestnut.

The plot revolves around a black father's struggle to raise his teenage son in the midst of drugs and gang violence in south central Los Angeles. Despite its antidrug, antiviolence message, the film sparked violence in several cities across the United States when it opened. A hit at the box office, it ultimately made more than $57 million.

July 20. An eighteen-year-old contestant in the Miss Black America pageant filed a complaint with the Indianapolis (Indiana) Police Department charging that former heavyweight champion Mike Tyson had raped her in his hotel room the night before. (Tyson had been in town promoting the pageant.) She also filed a $21 million sexual assault lawsuit. (Also see entries dated September 9, 1991, and February 10, 1992.)

July. Bishop James P. Lyke was installed as the new archbishop of Atlanta, Georgia, making him the nation's highest-ranking black Roman Catholic.

The fifty-two-year-old Lyke had been serving as administrator of the diocese ever since the summer of 1990, when Eugene Marino resigned from the post of archbishop after church officials learned of his affair with a young woman. (See entry dated July, 1990.) A native of Chicago, Illinois, Lyke was ordained a priest in 1966. He came to Atlanta from Cleveland, Ohio, where he had served as auxiliary bishop since 1979. (Also see entry dated December, 1992.)

August 19-22. Four days of rioting involving African Americans and orthodox Jews erupted in the Crown Heights section of New York City. One person was killed and at least 100 others were injured, including several policemen.

The riot began after Gavin Cato, a seven-year-old black child, was struck and killed by a car in the Crown Heights community. The car was part of a motorcade escorting Rabbi Menachem Schneerson, leader of an ultra-conservative Jewish group based in Crown Heights. Witnesses said the car went out of control before striking the child.

Shortly after the accident, angry blacks filled the streets of the area. More than a dozen black youths surrounded twenty-nine-year-old Yankel Rosenbaum, a student from Melbourne, Australia. They beat, kicked, and then fatally stabbed him in revenge for the black child's death, even though Rosenbaum had just been an innocent bystander.

Both deaths created an uproar throughout New York City. About 200 people marched on City Hall. New York mayor David Dinkins pleaded for calm and later announced a $10,000 reward for information leading to the conviction of Rosenbaum's murderer.

Of the many youths who were involved in the attack on Rosenbaum, only one, sixteen-year-old Lemrick Nelson, was charged with murder. The police said they had found a bloody knife in his possession and that Rosenbaum had identified Nelson as his killer. The police also said that Nelson later confessed to the crime. (Also see entry dated October 29, 1992.)

August. Plans were announced for a Negro Leagues Baseball Museum in Kansas City, Missouri, as a tribute to the men who played the game at a time when the major leagues excluded them.

The museum is supposed to be part of a black culture complex. The first phase is expected to open in early 1994. Proceeds from the museum will be used to cover

Clarence Thomas

pension, health, and other benefits for surviving members of the Negro Leagues.

September 9. In Indianapolis, Indiana, a grand jury charged boxer Mike Tyson with raping an eighteen-year-old Miss Black America contestant in July. (Also see entries dated July 20, 1991, and February 10, 1992.)

September 10-27. In Washington, D.C., the Senate Judiciary Committee began hearings to decide if Judge Clarence Thomas was a suitable candidate for the U.S. Supreme Court.

Ever since Thomas's nomination was announced on July 1, more and more African American and women's rights leaders had stepped forward to speak out against him. They feared that as a conservative who opposed abortion and affirmative action, he would not serve the best interests of the country. (Also see entries dated July 1, 1991, and October 6-15, 1991.)

September 28. Jazz legend Miles Davis died of pneumonia, respiratory failure, and stroke in Santa Monica, California. He was sixty-five years old.

Born in 1926, he was just a teenager when he began sitting in with musicians such as Charlie Parker and Dizzy Gillespie whenever they visited his hometown of St. Louis. After studying briefly at the Juilliard School of Music in New York City in the mid-1940s, Davis started playing regularly in local clubs and touring with several different bands. He formed his own group in the late 1940s, but it soon failed. He tried again in 1956 and this time met with success. That same year, he released his first record, *Miles Ahead.*

Perhaps the best jazz trumpeter in modern times, Davis liked to create new sounds and styles. During the 1950s and into the 1960s, for example, he introduced such forms as "cool jazz," hard bop, and jazz-rock. Later, he experimented with new forms of electrified jazz and funk. His brand of jazz was unique—sometimes haunting, sometimes melancholy, and virtually free of vibrato (a slight tremor caused by rapid variations in pitch). He always played for his own ear and often performed with his back to the audience. Davis also influenced a number of other highly regarded musicians, from saxophonists John Coltrane and Wayne Shorter to keyboardist Herbie Hancock and trumpeter Wynton Marsalis.

Miles Davis

Some of Davis's most notable albums include *The Miles Davis Chronicles, Birth of the Cool, Sketches of Spain, Kind of Blue, Blue Sorcerer, In a Silent Way, Bitches Brew, On the Corner, Star People,* and *Tutu.*

September. Virginia governor L. Douglas Wilder announced that he was planning to run for president of the United States. In 1989, he became the nation's first elected African American governor. (See entry dated November 7, 1989.)

October 6-15. Anita Hill, a law professor at the University of Oklahoma, testified before the Senate Judiciary Committee that Supreme Court nominee Clarence Thomas had sexually harassed her years earlier when they both worked at the U.S. Department of Education and the Equal Employment Opportunity Commission (EEOC).

Anita Hill

Hill's appearance before the committee, which was televised nationally October 11-14, set off tremendous debate. Many people wondered why she had waited so long to come forward with her story. Some of them questioned whether what she had to report was even an appropriate issue to consider when selecting a Supreme Court justice. Others criticized the members of the Senate Judiciary Committee for hesitating to look into Hill's charges as soon as they had first heard about them. Many of these people were left with doubts about Thomas's suitability as a justice.

The hearings brought out the issues of both race and gender (sex). Hill became a symbol for many working women. For many African American women in particular, however, her testimony revived an age-old problem—whether to be loyal to one's race or to one's gender.

The committee later voted to confirm Thomas for the Supreme Court. (Also see entries dated July 1, 1991, and September 10-27, 1991.)

October 11. Redd Foxx, well-known comedian and actor, died of a heart attack during a rehearsal for the television sitcom "The Royal Family."

Foxx was born John Elroy Sanford in St. Louis, Missouri, on December 9, 1924. He began his career performing in various musical groups, including the Bon-Bons, beginning in 1939. He then turned to stand-up comedy in 1941 and recorded numerous comedy albums over the next fifty years. From 1947 through 1951, he teamed up with fellow comedian Slappy White and performed in front of predominantly black audiences. His early routines often featured sex-oriented jokes and profanity.

Foxx's popularity began to soar during the 1970s. He made television history as the star of "Sanford & Son," which ran from 1972 to 1977 and can still be seen in syndication. He also starred in his own "Redd Foxx Comedy Hour," "Redd Foxx Show," and "The Royal Family." His movie credits include *Cotton Comes to Harlem, Norman ... Is That You?,* and *Harlem Nights.*

Foxx won a Golden Globe Award for his performance as best actor in a comedy and received three Emmy Award nominations for best actor in a comedy.

October 11. Former Washington, D.C., mayor Marion Barry began serving his six-month prison sentence for perjury and cocaine possession. He had been convicted in 1990.

The fifty-five-year-old Barry had served three terms as mayor of the District of Columbia. Some blacks believed FBI investigators targeted him because of his race and that he had been entrapped, or lured into a situation in which he ended up breaking the law. (Also see entries dated June 13, 1990; April, 1992; and September, 1992.)

November 7. Earvin "Magic" Johnson, an all-star guard for the Los Angeles Lakers, shocked the nation by announcing his retirement from the National Basketball Association (NBA) after he tested positive for HIV, the virus that causes AIDS.

November 29. Popular novelist Frank Yerby died in Madrid, Spain. During the 1940s and 1950s, he had specialized in a type of fiction that was unusual for black writers—historical tales of adventure and romance featuring daring heroes and ladies in danger.

Born on September 5, 1916, in Augusta, Georgia, Yerby received a bachelor's degree from Paine College in 1937 and a

Magic Johnson

307

master's degree from Fisk University in 1938. He taught college-level English for several years in Florida and Louisiana before heading north in 1941 to take a wartime factory job in Detroit, Michigan.

During this same period, Yerby also began writing. His first published short story, "Health Card," was a bitter tale of racial injustice. It won a special O. Henry Memorial Award in 1944.

Yerby then turned to producing historical fiction. In 1946, he published his first novel, *The Foxes of Harrow,* which took place on a southern plantation before the Civil War. (A year later, it was made into a hit movie starring Rex Harrison and Maureen O'Hara.) He returned again and again to this setting for many of his later stories and novels, which proved to be enormously popular with readers. Some of his other best-selling works were *The Golden Hawk, A Woman Called Fancy*, and *The Saracen Blade*.

Yerby was often the target of criticism for his choice of subject matter. Black reviewers condemned him for not addressing the problems of his race. Reviewers who did not know he was black accused him of wasting his writing talent on cardboard characters and overdone plots.

As the child of a racially mixed couple, Yerby responded by declaring: "I don't think a writer's output should be dictated by a biological accident. It happens there are many things I know far better than the race problem." Pointing out that his background was a mix of Scotch-Irish, Native American, and black, he explained, "I simply insist on remaining a member of the human race."

His own solution to the racial discrimination he experienced in the United States was to leave the country. Yerby spent the second half of his life in Europe, living first in France before settling permanently in Spain.

December 4. A Los Angeles judge sentenced white supremacist Tom Metzger to six months in jail, three years' probation, and 330 hours of community service working with minority groups for his part in a cross-burning incident in 1983. The two other men on trial with him received similar sentences. (Also see entry dated June 23, 1991.)

December. Nine people were trampled to death during a celebrity basketball game featuring rap artists Heavy D and Michael Bivens at the City College of New York.

The event created an uproar among critics of rap music, who claim there is a connection between rap music and violence. (Also see entries dated December 26, 1992; and June 8, 1993.)

1992   **January 2.** W. Wilson Goode's term as mayor of Philadelphia, Pennsylvania, ended with the inauguration of Ed Rendell. Goode had served eight years (from 1984 until 1992) as the city's first black mayor.

During his time in office, there was enough new office construction to change the Philadelphia skyline. Goode also helped promote African American business. Before he left office, for example, there were four black-owned shopping centers, three of which had been built while he was mayor.

While Goode brought more business and financial strength to the city, some critics believe that such positive contributions were overshadowed by his conflicts with MOVE, a predominantly black "back to nature" group. In May, 1985, the mayor approved a police plan to bomb a house where MOVE members had been involved in a day-long shootout with law enforcement officials. The bomb touched off a fire that killed eleven people (including four children) and destroyed two blocks of houses, leaving several hundred people homeless. MOVE members and residents of the neighborhood who lost their homes always held Goode responsible for the incident. An investigation later in the year showed that various city departments had mishandled the crisis.

January 25. At Grammy Award ceremonies in New York City, James Brown, the renowned "Godfather of Soul," received an Award of Merit for his lifetime contribution to music.

Brown was born in 1934 and grew up in Augusta, Georgia. He was twenty-two when he formed his own group, and he has rarely stopped performing since then. Brown's imprint is on virtually every black musical movement since the 1950s. He is credited with influencing soul, funk, disco, and rap, either with his songwriting or with his distinctive gravelly voice.

Brown's performing style is unique, too. His act is marked by screams, wails, grunts, moans, and dramatic body movements. Many rock and rap singers have copied his style or have used parts of his recordings (a technique known as "sampling") in their own songs.

Brown has had ninety-four songs in the top 100 and more top-20 singles than any other musician in history. Only the late Elvis Presley has appeared more often on the pop charts. Among Brown's biggest hits are "Please, Please, Please," "Try Me," "Out of Sight," "Papa's Got a Brand New Bag," "Say It Loud—I'm Black and I'm Proud," "I Got You (I Feel Good)," and "Living in America."

Brown has also made news for his encounters with police. In 1972, for example, he made national headlines when he was arrested and charged with disorderly conduct in Knoxville, Tennessee. He claimed he had been talking to some children about the dangers of drugs and dropping out of school, but the police accused him of creating a scene and failing to move on after they had ordered him to do so. Another highly publicized incident took place in the late 1980s, when Brown was arrested for leading police on a high-speed chase through two states. Convicted in 1989, he was sentenced to a six-year jail term. In February, 1991, however, he was freed early for good behavior and ordered to take part in a special work-release program.

January 29. Willie Dixon, a musician considered one of the greatest traditional bluesmen, died in Burbank, California. He was seventy-six years old.

Dixon created lusty and sometimes humorous songs full of suggestive images and lyrics. He began recording in 1940 and wrote more than 300 songs, including such blues standards as "Hoochie Coochie Man," "Little Red Rooster," "The Seventh Son," and "Bring It on Home." He also wrote "You Can't Judge a Book by Its Cover," "Built for Comfort," and "Wang Dang Doodle."

Although many of Dixon's songs were hits, they were often more closely associated with musicians other than him. He wrote many of his best pieces for such performers as Howlin' Wolf, Bo Diddley, and Muddy Waters. Others were made famous by various rock groups, including the Rolling Stones, Led Zeppelin, the Grateful Dead, and the Yardbirds.

January. The rap group Public Enemy released its song "By the Time I Get to Arizona" to celebrate Martin Luther King, Jr.'s birthday. The video version created a nationwide controversy because it showed the burning of an Arizona state trooper's car. This revived angry feelings about Arizona's failure to make King's birthday a state holiday. (Also see entries dated January 18, 1988; November 6, 1990; and January 18, 1993.)

February 10. In Indianapolis, Indiana, a jury convicted heavyweight boxing champion Mike Tyson of raping an eighteen-year-old beauty-pageant contestant. (See entries dated July 20, 1991, and September 9, 1991.) He was later sentenced to six years in a federal prison.

February 10. Alex Haley, author of *Roots: The Saga of an American Family* and *The Autobiography of Malcolm X*, died of a heart attack in Seattle, Washington.

Haley was born on August 11, 1921, in Ithaca, New York. As a child, he spent his summer vacations in Henning, Tennessee, at the home of his maternal grandparents. There he passed many hours on his grandmother's front porch listening to her and her sisters tell exciting stories about an African ancestor named "Kin-tay."

More than forty years later, Haley became the first African American to win literary fame for bringing his family history to life. Published during America's bicentennial in 1976, *Roots: The Saga of an American Family* vividly traced Haley's ancestry back seven generations to its beginnings in West Africa. The book was the product of more than twelve years of extensive genealogical research that spanned three continents.

Roots won a special Pulitzer Prize, a National Book Award, and nearly 300 other honors. In 1977, it became the basis of one of television's most popular miniseries, an eight-part program watched by more than 130 million people. (That was two-thirds of the possible audience, which was then a record.) By taking a frank look at the birth of the United States and the slavery era, the book as well as the miniseries sparked passionate debates about race relations in America.

Haley was famous for his exhaustive research and attention to detail even before *Roots*. In 1965, for example, after a year of intense interviews with Malcolm X, the Black Muslim leader, Haley published *The Autobiography of Malcolm X*. An enduring bestseller, it eventually became the inspiration for black filmmaker Spike Lee's movie biography of Malcolm X.

During his long career, Haley also contributed stories, articles and interviews to *Playboy, Harper's,* the *Atlantic Monthly,* and *Reader's Digest.* At the time of his death, he was working on a number of different projects, including the script for "Queen," a new television miniseries about his father's family. (Also see entries dated February 3, 1977; March 14, 1977; May 19, 1977; September 11, 1977; November 18, 1992; and February 14, 1993.)

February 15. Benjamin Hooks, executive director of the NAACP, announced his retirement from the organization he had served since succeeding Roy Wilkins in 1977. Under his leadership, the NAACP's membership had grown to 500,000, making it one of the largest black institutions in the United States.

A native of Memphis, Tennessee, Hooks attended LeMoyne College and Howard University before receiving a law degree from DePaul University in 1948. Returning to Memphis, Hooks served as an assistant public defender and later became the first black judge to serve in the Shelby County Criminal Court. He was also active in the local business community as co-founder and vice-president of the Mutual Federal Savings and Loan Association from 1955 until 1969.

Hooks first gained national attention in 1972 as the first black member of the Federal Communications Commission (FCC). In that position, he worked hard to expand employment and ownership opportunities for blacks in radio and television and also tried to change the way blacks were portrayed in the media.

Hooks is also an ordained Baptist minister with ties to churches in Memphis as well as in Detroit, Michigan.

March. NBN Broadcasting Inc. and Sheridan Broadcasting Network, the nation's two largest black-owned radio network companies, merged to form the American Urban Radio Networks. The new company provides programming to five radio networks that serve approximately 300 stations nationally. It also owns three other network organizations—STRZ Entertainment Network, SBN Sports Network, and SPM Radio Network. (Also see entry dated July 2, 1973.)

April. After serving a six-month sentence for possession of cocaine, former District of Columbia mayor Marion Barry was released from federal prison.

About 300 of his most faithful supporters celebrated the occasion with a reception and luncheon. At the party, Barry told well-wishers that he had "re-established" his relationship with God while he was behind bars. As a result, he declared, "I come out of prison better and not bitter." (Also see entries dated June 13, 1990; October 11, 1991; and September, 1992.)

April 7. Tennis star Arthur Ashe confirmed rumors that he was infected with the AIDS virus.

Ashe had first learned of his condition in 1988 when he was about to undergo brain surgery. He apparently contracted the disease through blood transfusions he had received during open-heart surgery in 1983. In order to protect his family, he told only a few people that he had AIDS. But when a reporter for *USA Today* contacted him to say that the newspaper was going to run a story about his health, Ashe decided to go public with the news himself. (Also see entries dated July 5, 1975, and February 6, 1993.)

April 29-May 1. In Alameda County, California, a jury acquitted four Los Angeles police officers who had been captured on videotape beating black motorist Rodney King. They had been charged with using excessive force. (See entries dated March 3-5, 1991, and March 14, 1991.)

Within hours, their acquittal sparked the most severe riot in U.S. history. It took place in predominantly black south central Los Angeles. There, black youths brutally beat white motorists who drove through the area, and rioters burned and

Rodney King meets with reporters to plead for calm during the Los Angeles riots

looted stores and other businesses. President George Bush called for calm and sent federal troops to the area, promising to take whatever measures proved necessary to end the violence.

While the outcome of the Rodney King trial was the immediate cause of the disturbance, it was not the only source of anger and frustration in south central Los Angeles. Some blacks were also upset about relations between blacks and Koreans in the city.

In fact, many of the stores rioters destroyed were owned by Korean Americans. The black residents claimed that the Korean merchants were impolite and treated black shoppers as if they were going to shoplift. (They pointed to an earlier incident in particular in which a black girl was shot and killed by a Korean store owner who suspected her of shoplifting.) Fearing for their lives and disappointed over the lack of police protection during the riot, some Korean merchants armed themselves and fired at would-be looters.

Blacks, whites, and Asians all believe that the police did not act quickly enough to stop the rioting. They also blame the slow response of authorities for the property destruction, which was estimated in the billions of dollars. Early reports from the Los Angeles coroner's office indicated that fifty-eight people died during the disturbance. This figure was later revised to fifty-three, but this was still enough to make it the deadliest riot in U.S. history. (See entries dated May 2, 1992, and October 22, 1992.)

While Los Angeles burned, rioting also broke out in several other major U.S. cities, causing federal officials to fear that a national crisis was about to erupt. Atlanta, Georgia, Seattle, Washington, and New York City all experienced violence. But it was another California city, San Francisco, that suffered more damage than any place outside of Los Angeles. Rioters there damaged more than 100 downtown businesses, and police arrested over 1,500 people.

May 2. Los Angeles mayor Tom Bradley welcomed federal troops as the residents of the south central section of the city began cleaning up the debris after three days of rioting.

Over 20,000 federal troops, National Guard troops, federal agents, and police from neighboring cities had been sent to the area to restore and maintain order. More than 2,000 people had been injured, and the death total continued to climb. Rioters had destroyed 3,800 buildings and left 10,000 other structures burned, vandalized, or looted. Property damage was estimated at more than $550 million. President George Bush declared the riot-torn neighborhoods a disaster area, making them eligible for special federal aid.

Former baseball commissioner Peter Ueberroth, who had managed the city's preparations for the 1984 Summer Olympics, accepted Mayor Bradley's invitation to direct the rebuilding effort in Los Angeles. (Also see entry dated October 22, 1992.)

May 2. Dance Floor, a horse owned by rap artist M.C. Hammer and his family, finished third in the Kentucky Derby. Hammer is believed to be the first African American to enter a horse in the Kentucky Derby, the first of three important contests in the so-called Triple Crown of thoroughbred racing.

June 30. Willie L. Williams, former police commissioner of Philadelphia, Pennsylvania, became the first black police chief in Los Angeles, California. He replaced the controversial Darryl Gates, who was the head of the department at the time of the Rodney King beating in March, 1991, and also during the riot that followed the April, 1992, acquittal of the four officers charged in the incident.

Political infighting, community distrust, and low morale had plagued the Los Angeles Police Department ever since the Rodney King beating made international headlines. (Also see entries dated March 3-5, 1991; March 14, 1991; April 4-8, 1991; July 9, 1991; and April 29-May 1, 1992.)

July 28. At the urging of his record company, Time Warner, rap artist Ice-T removed the song "Cop Killer" from his *Body Count* album.

Critics condemned the action, saying it paved the way for the censorship of rap. They were especially angry with Time Warner. They accused the company of giving in under pressure from politicians and special interest groups after promising to support Ice-T's First Amendment rights to freedom of speech.

September 12. Thirty-five-year-old Mae Jemison, a physician and scientist, was one of seven astronauts aboard the space shuttle *Endeavor* as it blasted off for a

Mae Jemison

seven-day mission. She was the first African American woman in space. (Also see entry dated March, 1993.)

September. Less than six months after being released from prison, former District of Columbia mayor Marion Barry won a city council seat in Washington's Democratic primary election.

In an upset victory that shocked many observers, he defeated longtime black councilwoman Wilhelmina Rolark. She had represented one of the city's poorest and most crime-ridden districts for four terms and had been endorsed for re-election by local newspapers, civic groups, and Washington, D.C., mayor Sharon Pratt Kelly. (Also see entries dated June 13, 1990; October 11, 1991; and April, 1992.)

October 5. Eddie Kendrick, the melodic tenor behind most of the Temptations' biggest hits, died of lung cancer at the age of fifty-two. He had lost a lung to the disease eleven months earlier.

Kendrick set the standard for falsetto singing (that is, using an artificially high-pitched voice) and helped to launch such Temptations hits as "Get Ready," "The Way You Do the Things You Do," and "Just My Imagination" to the top of the Pop and R&B charts. With Kendrick as their lead singer, the Temptations became one of the nation's most popular and successful male groups. They had thirteen top-ten hits during the eleven years he spent as a Temptation.

Kendrick left the group in the early 1970s for a solo career and soon topped the music charts with the hit "Keep On Trucking." In 1982, he rejoined the Temptations for a brief reunion tour.

October 6. Alarmed by an earlier attack on a black student, minority students at the University of Massachusetts occupied offices of a campus building in protest.

They also asked school officials to set aside Columbus Day as a time to study discrimination against non-white societies.

The racial turmoil had begun on September 25 after a black dormitory assistant was attacked by a white man who allegedly punched him and shouted racial insults. The assistant later found feces dumped outside his room and racial slurs written on his door. (Also see entry dated February 19, 1988.)

October 11. Prince, a musician known for his provocative rock songs and equally daring outfits, made a deal with Warner Brothers Records that guaranteed him the highest amount of money ever paid to a recording artist.

Under the terms of his contract, Prince, who is also a composer and producer for other singers and musicians, could earn a $10 million advance for each of his next six albums provided the previous album sells more than five million copies. He was also named a company vice-president. (Also see entries dated February 26, 1985, and June, 1993.)

October 15. The name and certain assets of the 118-year-old *Oakland Tribune*, the nation's only major black-owned daily newspaper, were sold to a California-based company known as the Alameda Newspaper Group. Excluded from the deal were the newspaper's presses and its landmark headquarters building.

The *Tribune* had become a symbol of racial pride when Robert C. Maynard, a well-respected columnist with the *Washington Post*, and his wife, Nancy Hicks, a noted journalist with the *Boston Globe*, bought it from the Gannett Company. At the time of the purchase, African Americans represented less than 10 percent of the staffs of the nation's newspapers. So having blacks own the *Tribune* held out hope for African American success in mainstream publishing.

Despite their efforts to streamline costs, Maynard and Hicks continually faced financial problems with the struggling newspaper. That made it especially hard for them to compete with other papers in the San Francisco Bay/San Jose area. Eventually, selling the *Tribune* became the only solution. (Also see entry dated November 4, 1992.)

October 22. The 222-page Webster Commission report on the Los Angeles riots of April, 1992, blasted former police chief Darryl Gates for not handling the conflict properly. It also recommended ways to avoid future disturbances.

The Webster Commission was an investigative group headed by the FBI and CIA chief William Webster. Members of the commission spent several months studying the violence that erupted after the controversial verdicts in the Rodney King trial.

In their report, the commissioners blamed Chief Gates for failing to come up with an effective plan to control the disorder, including providing meaningful training for Los Angeles Police Department officers. The report also pointed out that political squabbles had paralyzed city officials at the very time they needed to show some unity. "Gates had a responsibility to protect citizens," Webster declared. "There was too little help and it came too late."

Less than two months after the riots, Gates had retired from the police department and taken a job as a radio talk show host. According to an article in *USA Today*, he was very angry about the commission's report and responded by saying, "We should've blown a few heads off. Maybe that would have stopped it." Gates insisted that he had had a good plan that was carried out poorly.

The commission also recommended ways to avoid future riots. Members interviewed more than 400 residents, police officers, and city officials to come up with suggestions that are expected to serve as a model for riot response in other areas of the country. Some of their recommendations include increasing police patrols on city streets, upgrading outdated emergency communications systems (including 911), developing a riot-response plan before controversial trials end, and improving coordination and cooperation among city officials.

October 28. Actor/comedian Bill Cosby, an outspoken critic of the image of blacks on television, made a bid to purchase the National Broadcasting Company (NBC).

People familiar with the industry believed he was one of six candidates who were interested in buying the financially struggling network, which was losing the television ratings war against rivals CBS and ABC. The selling price was rumored to be $3.5 billion. Cosby said he would make the deal in an arrangement involving two close friends in the industry. He also said that he would not run the network himself.

During the late 1980s, Cosby had helped boost NBC from the number-three to the number-one spot with his ground-breaking series "The Cosby Show," which debuted in 1984. (He was its creator as well as its star.) The situation comedy about

Cast of "The Cosby Show"

middle-class African American life shot to the top of the ratings and held that position for a record number of years. It featured Cosby as an obstetrician and Phylicia Rashad as his wife, an attorney. Cosby himself ended the show after the 1991-1992 season to devote himself to several new projects. (Also see entry dated June, 1993.)

October 29. The New York State Supreme Court acquitted Lemrick Nelson of the August 19, 1991, stabbing death of an Australian rabbinical student during a riot in the Crown Heights section of New York City.

Nelson's acquittal sparked a new round of protests from Jewish residents of New York. On October 31, the U.S. Justice Department announced that it would investigate Rosenbaum's death. (Also see entry dated August 19-22, 1991.)

October 30. James Walker, a lead singer with the Dixie Hummingbirds, one of the country's best-known gospel quartets, died at his home in Philadelphia, Pennsylvania. He was sixty-six.

A native of Mileston, Mississippi, Walker joined the Dixie Hummingbirds in 1954. Before that, he had served in the Navy and worked with other singing groups. Gifted with a powerful tenor voice and an appealing personality, he eventually became one of the Hummingbirds' most popular members. Walker also composed more than seventy of the group's songs.

October. Cito Gaston, manager of the Toronto Blue Jays since 1989, became the first African American to manage a team to a Major League Baseball World Series championship. Toronto defeated the Atlanta Braves, the team that had been favored to win. This made the Blue Jays the first non-U.S. team to enter and win the World Series.

Gaston had begun his major league career in 1967 with the Atlanta Braves of the National League. In 1968 he was traded to the San Diego Padres. He played six years with the Padres and then returned to Atlanta before being traded to the Pittsburgh Pirates in 1977. After being dropped by the Pirates in 1979, Gaston played two years in the Dominican League and the Mexican League before retiring from baseball.

Gaston emerged from retirement in 1981 as a minor league hitting coach for the Atlanta Braves. He took a similar position with the Toronto Blue Jays in 1982 that eventually led to his promotion to team manager.

November 2. NBA superstar Earvin "Magic" Johnson announced that he was quitting basketball for good after making a brief comeback.

Johnson had originally retired from the Los Angeles Lakers in 1991 after learning he was a carrier of HIV, the virus that causes AIDS. (See entry dated November 7, 1991.) He had been afraid that the demands of a professional athletic career might be too hard on his health. But after a successful stint as a member of the 1992 U.S. Olympic team, Johnson decided to give the sport another try. He rejoined the Lakers for the 1992-1993 season with the idea of playing in at least fifty games.

Johnson's return to basketball was greeted with mixed reactions from NBA officials, players, and fans. Several players, for example, were afraid that they might catch AIDS from Johnson while on the court. And at least one team owner suggested that his retirement had been in everyone's best interest. Upset by all the controversy, Johnson chose to end his career.

November 3. Arkansas governor Bill Clinton won a lopsided election victory over President George Bush and independent candidate H. Ross Perot. Much of Clinton's support came from black voters and discontented middle-class whites who had suffered from the effects of a long-lasting recession that left thousands of workers hitting the unemployment lines.

Some political analysts suggested that Clinton gained black support partly because he managed to bring together different groups of people—such as gays, women's rights activists, and African Americans—who had decided they needed a change from the previous presidential administration and Republican leadership. Many hoped that he would fill important Cabinet, Supreme Court, and other federal agency positions with women, African Americans, and members of other groups that were not widely represented in government. They also hoped that his election would bring more domestic programs to help the economy and improve life in the cities.

The president-elect's transition team, which he began assembling almost immediately after the election, included several African American men and women. Heading the team was Vernon Jordan, who had been active in the business world since leaving his post as executive director of the Urban League. (He shared the top spot with Warren Christopher, Clinton's senior policy advisor.) Among the others the president-elect turned to for advice were Barbara Jordan, former Democratic representative and currently a college professor; William Gray III, former Democratic representative who now heads the United Negro College Fund; Marian Wright Edelman, founding president of the Children's Defense Fund; and Joycelyn Elders, head of Arkansas's human resources department.

Carol Moseley-Braun

November 3. Forty-five-year-

321

old Democrat Carol Moseley-Braun became the nation's first black female senator when she defeated Republican Richard Williamson, a Chicago lawyer. She was the first African American in the U.S. Senate since Republican Edward Brooke of Massachusetts lost his seat in 1979.

In other significant election results, Alan Page, a National Football League Hall of Fame defensive lineman, was elected to a six-year term on the Minnesota Supreme Court. This made him the first African American to hold an elective statewide office in Minnesota. In Illinois, Bobby Rush was elected to the U.S. House of Representatives. He was a former Black Panther Party leader who later served as deputy chairman of the Illinois Democratic Party and as a Chicago alderman. And in Florida, Alcee Hastings, a former federal judge impeached by Congress in 1989 on bribery and perjury charges, was also elected to the U.S. House of Representatives. (See entries dated March 16, 1989, and October 20, 1989.) His victory came not long after a federal judge ruled that his impeachment was unconstitutional because only a Senate committee and not the full Senate had heard his case.

Reports by the Senate Historian, House Historian, Congressional Black Caucus, Congressional Hispanic Caucus, and *Congressional Quarterly* revealed that there were now more minorities in Congress. A record number of minorities ran for Congress in 1992 and won, making the House and the Senate more reflective of the nation's population than ever before in history.

November 4. Pearl Stewart, a longtime journalist in the San Francisco Bay area, was named the new editor of the *Oakland Tribune*. She thus became the first African American woman to head a major metropolitan daily newspaper. (Also see entry dated October 15, 1992.)

November 9. The Johnson Publishing Company, publishers of *Jet, Ebony,* and *EM* magazines, celebrated its fiftieth anniversary.

John H. Johnson formed his company in 1942 to publish magazines for an audience that white publications did not reach. He got the idea for his first magazine, *Negro Digest*, while putting together a weekly summary of black-oriented news for the president of a black-owned insurance company. Unable to convince friends to support his dream of creating his own magazine of black news, he took out a $500 loan. He then contacted 20,000 people on the insurance company's mailing list and asked them to send him $2 if they liked the idea of a monthly magazine that focused on black news. Three thousand people responded to his letter, and *Negro Digest* was born. A year later, it had a readership of 50,000 people.

The key to the company's growth, however, was *Ebony* magazine. Founded in 1945, it was modeled after *Life* magazine. By 1992, *Ebony* was the largest circulating magazine published for blacks, boasting a readership of over 1.8 million people.

Over the years, the Johnson Publishing Company has become a model for other black-owned businesses. The company and its founder have been credited with helping change the way blacks view themselves. Through his magazines, Johnson helped blacks build self-esteem, learn about others, follow black news, and realize that African Americans can enjoy a satisfying lifestyle and achieve top professional goals.

In addition to producing magazines, the Johnson Publishing Company owns the Fashion Fair line of cosmetics for black women, the nationally syndicated TV show "Ebony-Jet Showcase," a travel agency, and three radio stations.

November 13. Riddick Bowe defeated Evander Holyfield in a twelve-round unanimous decision to claim the title of undisputed heavyweight boxing champion. Holyfield had held the title ever since former champion Mike Tyson was forced to give it up following his conviction on rape charges earlier in the year.

November 16. In Detroit, Michigan, two white police officers were charged with murder and a black officer was charged with manslaughter in the death of black motorist Malice Green.(The charges against the black officer were later dismissed.) A fourth officer was also charged in the assault, and three other officers were suspended but not charged.

The thirty-five-year-old Green, a Detroit resident, died of head wounds after being beaten by officers on November 5. The incident occurred near a suspected drug house.

Green's death sparked an outcry in Detroit, where people compared it to the 1991 police beating of black Los Angeles motorist Rodney King. (See entry dated March 3-5, 1991.) In Detroit, however, both the African American mayor, Coleman Young, and the African American police chief, Stanley Knox, quickly condemned the beating and took swift action against the officers involved. (Also see entry dated June 18, 1993.)

November 18. Director Spike Lee's epic motion picture *Malcolm X* opened nationwide. Starring Oscar-winning actor Denzel Washington, the $34 million film was based on the slain Black Muslim leader's autobiography. (See entries dated March 12, 1964, and February 21, 1965.)

From the very start, the project was controversial. Some blacks wondered if Spike Lee would be able to do justice to the life of Malcolm X. Hollywood executives were reluctant to support a film about a militant black activist who has become best known for his declaration that African Americans must defend themselves and achieve racial equality "by any means necessary." The executives also hesitated at the proposed length of the movie (more than three hours) and the cost.

However, Lee argued successfully that Oliver Stone's recent film on President John F. Kennedy—a difficult subject like Malcolm X—had run longer than the average movie. And when money for the project ran low, a number of African American entertainers, sports figures, and others came to Lee's rescue with enough financial backing to see him through the two years it took to make *Malcolm X.*

During the course of documenting Malcolm's "life-changing" 1964 pilgrimage to the Middle East, Lee became the first Hollywood filmmaker to be granted permission to film the annual gathering in the Saudi Arabian city of Mecca, Islam's holiest city. Other scenes were shot in New York, Egypt, and the Republic of South Africa.

For the most part, critics looked favorably on the film. A few pointed out that Lee left out certain facts and changed others, such as ignoring how important Malcolm's sister Ella was in his life. (Among other things, she was the one who helped pay for his trip to Mecca.) Many others praised *Malcolm X* as an epic motion picture comparable to such films as *Lawrence of Arabia* and *Gandhi.*

The screening of *Malcolm X* was an event of major significance for many African Americans, especially young people. They have raised Malcolm's stature in recent years to the point where he rivals Martin Luther King, Jr., in their eyes. His fiery speeches, in which he rejected nonviolence as a way of life in the human rights struggle, are very appealing to many disillusioned blacks in the 1990s.

November 24. Henry "Hank" Aaron, vice-president of the Atlanta Braves baseball team and the sport's all-time leading home-run hitter, urged Major League Baseball officials to suspend Cincinnati Reds owner Marge Schott for using racial slurs against blacks and Jews.

Her racist remarks had first become public in documents related to a lawsuit filed by a former Reds employee. Then others stepped forward to say that they, too, had heard her use terms such as "million-dollar niggers" and "money-grubbing Jews."

Schott responded to the outcry against her by denying she is racist. But, she added, "If I have said anything to offend anyone, it was never my intention and I apologize for any hurt it may have caused." Her insensitivity nevertheless prompted many current and former black players, national black leaders (including Jesse Jackson), and others to demand that she be punished in some way. (Also see entries dated December 7, 1992, and February 3, 1993.)

November. The Harvard Law School established the Reginald F. Lewis International Law Center, thanks to a $3 million grant from the Reginald F. Lewis Foundation. It was the largest gift in the 175-year history of the school.

The Lewis Foundation is a charitable organization supported by the personal contributions of Reginald Lewis, an African American business executive and financier who graduated from Harvard. Lewis heads the New York-based TLC Beatrice International Holidings Inc. (Also see entry dated January 19, 1993.)

November. The Shoney's restaurant chain proposed a settlement in a racial discrimination lawsuit that employees and job applicants had filed back in 1989. (See entry dated October 6, 1989.) The largest class-action lawsuit of its kind, it involved as many as 80,000 people and $105 million in damages.

Shoney's co-founder and major stockholder, Raymond L. Danner, had been accused in the lawsuit of using racial slurs and reprimanding managers if they had what he thought were too many black employees. He did not deny these claims, and shortly after the news of the settlement was made public, he sold all of his stock in the company and left the board of directors.

December 7. As Major League Baseball's winter meetings began in Louisville, Kentucky, team owners took up the case of Cincinnati Reds owner Marge Schott and her alleged use of racial slurs. (See entry dated November 24, 1992.)

During the meetings, Schott once again apologized publicly for her remarks, declaring, "I know in my heart that I am not a racist or bigot." Meanwhile, a four-person investigating committee began considering the charges against her. Jesse Jackson also met with several team owners to discuss racism in baseball and push for improved hiring opportunities for minorities. he suggested that blacks might boycott the game if owners did not take steps to address the problems. (Also see entry dated February 3, 1993.)

December 7. While on a goodwill tour of Japan, some members of Texas Southern University's famous Ocean of Soul Marching Band went on a shoplifting spree in Tokyo. Japanese police estimated that the students took about $22,000 worth of electronic equipment. The Americans were not allowed to leave the country until the items were returned.

In the weeks after the incident, embarrassed officials of the historically black university responded by abolishing the group and suspending twelve band members. The suspended students were eventually allowed to return to school, but they remained on probation. They were also required to take a class in ethics, which studies the principles of good versus bad and their effect on behavior.

December 12. In Montgomery, Alabama, black legislators boycotted rededication ceremonies for the state capitol to protest Governor Guy Hunt's insistence on flying the Confederate flag over the remodeled building.

The legislators had argued for years that the rebel flag is offensive to blacks and others because it is a symbol of racial oppression and hatred. But the governor refused to listen to their protests and continued to fly the flag. (Also see entries dated January 31, 1988, and January, 1993.)

December 12. President-elect Bill Clinton named the first black to his cabinet—fifty-one-year-old Ron Brown as secretary of commerce.

A Washington-based attorney and lobbyist, Brown had been serving as the chairman of the Democratic National Committee since 1988. (He was the first black in the party's top-ranking position.) Before that, he served as deputy campaign manager to Senator Edward Kennedy of Massachusetts during his 1980 bid for the

Democratic presidential nomination and as convention manager to Jesse Jackson during the 1988 presidential campaign.

December 15. In Nashville, Tennessee, two white policemen were fired for allegedly beating up a black motorist who turned out to be a fellow officer from their own precinct who was working on an undercover investigation.

The incident occurred when five white officers tried to stop Reggie Miller for driving an unmarked police vehicle with an expired license tag. To avoid ruining his investigation, he tried to lead them a few blocks out of the neighborhood so that they could talk. Then, according to Miller, they kicked, beat, and choked him before he was finally able to convince them that he was a policeman, too.

The fired officers insisted their treatment of Miller was not racially motivated and immediately announced their intention to appeal the decision to dismiss them from the force.

December 16. The Mississippi Supreme Court paved the way for seventy-two-year-old Byron de la Beckwith to be to be tried a third time for the 1963 murder of civil rights leader Medgar Evers. (See entry dated June 12, 1963.)

Beckwith had been tried twice for the crime back in 1964. In both instances, all-white juries could not reach a verdict. Charges against the admitted white supremacist were finally dropped in 1969.

Mississippi authorities reopened the case in 1989 and discovered enough new evidence to arrest and charge Beckwith again in December, 1990. He then argued that he had been denied his constitutional right to a fair and speedy trial. But the state supreme court justices eventually turned down his request to have the charges against him dismissed on those grounds. Their decision left it up to the state circuit court judge to set a new trial date for Beckwith.

December 18. "Mother" Clara Hale, who established an internationally known care program for drug-addicted and AIDS-infected babies who had been abandoned or orphaned, died in New York City of complications from a stroke. She was eighty-seven.

A native of North Carolina, Hale headed north with her family to Philadelphia, Pennsylvania, as a young girl. Orphaned at the age of sixteen, she later married

Thomas Hale and moved with him to New York City. After her husband died and left her with three young children to support, Hale went to work as a cleaning woman. She then began caring for neighborhood children in her home so that she could be with her own sons and daughter all day. She became a licensed foster parent in 1940 and successfully raised about forty children over the next thirty years.

In 1969, Hale was just about ready to retire from being a foster parent when she took over the care of a baby who was born to a drug-addicted mother. Word soon spread that she had nursed the infant through withdrawal symptoms free of charge, and within just a few months some twenty-two other drug-addicted babies were sleeping in cribs near Mother Hale's own bed.

Hale House, as her care program came to be known, has since taken in more than 1,000 sick babies, including ones infected with HIV and AIDS. The kind and devoted head of the house personally tended to as many of them as possible until her age and health left her too weak to hold them anymore. "I'm simply a person who loves children," Hale once explained. "We hold them and touch them. They love you to tell them how great they are, how good they are. Somehow, even at a young age, they understand that. They're happy, and they turn out well."

Hale's pioneering efforts are expected to continue under the sponsorship of the Hale Foundation.

December 21. Famed blues guitarist Albert King, who influenced a generation of rock guitarists such as Eric Clapton and Stevie Ray Vaughan, died of a heart attack in Memphis, Tennessee. He was sixty-nine.

Born in Mississippi, King began his music career as a drummer and later switched to guitar. Although he was left-handed, he played a right-handed guitar and developed a unique style of pulling rather than pushing the strings. His first big hits came during the mid-1960s, when he performed with Booker T. and the MGs on blues standards such as "Born under a Bad Sign" and "Laundromat Blues."

December 26. In Seattle, Washington, a small riot broke out after a concert featuring rapper Ice Cube. Four people were shot and three others injured during the disturbance, which also led the arrests of nearly fifty people.

Many observers blamed Ice Cube for provoking the crowd with his music, which included raps dealing with racism, police violence, and using guns to frighten or kill. (Also see entries dated December, 1991, and June 8, 1993.)

December. Archbishop James P. Lyke, the highest-ranking black Roman Catholic in the United States, died of cancer at his home in Atlanta, Georgia. (Also see entry dated July, 1991.)

December. Star African American outfielder Barry Bonds signed a contract with the San Francisco Giants that made him the highest-paid player in the history of baseball. Under the terms of the deal, he was scheduled to receive $43.75 million over six years.

December. President-elect Bill Clinton named three more blacks to his cabinet— Jesse Brown as secretary of veterans affairs, Mike Espy as secretary of agriculture, and Joycelyn Elders as surgeon general.

The forty-eight-year-old Brown, a Vietnam veteran, was left with a partially paralyzed right arm as a result of wounds he suffered in combat. He served in the Marine Corps from 1963 until 1966 and then went to work for Disabled American Veterans. At the time of his nomination, Brown was in charge of the organization's Washington, D.C., office.

Espy, a thirty-nine-year-old member of the U.S. House of Representatives from Mississippi, had been one of the first blacks to endorse Clinton's run for the presidency. His interest in agriculture dated back to childhood, when he watched his father, a federal crop agent, try to help southern black farmers victimized by Jim Crowism. If confirmed, he would be the first black as well as the first southerner to serve as secretary of agriculture.

The fifty-nine-year-old Elders had worked with Governor Clinton in Arkansas since 1987 as his top health official. A pediatrician, she earned a reputation in her home state as a strong advocate for children and teenagers. Elders stirred up a major controversy there for opening school-based health clinics that passed out birth control information and devices to students on demand.

1993   **January 1.** Near Tampa, Florida, a vacationing black man was kidnapped by three white men, robbed, drenched with gasoline, and set on fire. His attackers left behind a misspelled note reading, "One les nigger, one more to go. KKK."

Thirty-one-year-old Christopher Wilson, a Jamaican immigrant from New York City, had gone out early New Year's morning to buy a newspaper. As he stopped at a shopping center, he was confronted by three men and forced at gunpoint to drive to a remote area. There he was taunted with racial slurs, assaulted, and left for dead. But he managed to make his way to a nearby home where a resident hosed him down with water. According to police, when they arrived on the scene, Wilson was in so much pain that he begged them to shoot him.

Although he suffered severe burns over 40 percent of his body, Wilson survived and was able to identify one of the men police later arrested, twenty-six-year-old Mark Kohut. Also arrested were Charles Rourk, age thirty-three, and Jeff Ray Pellett, age seventeen. Authorities described all three men as drifters who had met each other through a day-labor service. They were charged with carjacking (a federal crime), attempted murder, robbery, and kidnapping, for which they faced up to twenty-five years in prison. And since the case was officially classified as a hate crime because the attackers had referred to race as a motive, they faced even more jail time for violating Wilson's civil rights. (Also see entry dated June 7, 1993.)

Dizzy Gillespie

January 6. Jazz trumpeter Dizzy Gillespie, who helped create the revolutionary bebop style as well as Afro-Cuban jazz, died of pancreatic cancer in a New Jersey hospital at the age of seventy-five. His trademark bulging cheeks, bent horn, and fun-loving showmanship had entertained audiences throughout the world for over fifty years.

Born John Birks Gillespie in South Carolina in 1917, he first fell in love with the trumpet when he was in the third grade.

(Before that, he had studied piano.) He taught himself how to play it and was working professionally as a musician by his mid-teens. He had acquired his nickname, Dizzy, by then, too, as a result of his reputation for wearing odd clothing and clowning around on stage.

In the late 1930s, Gillespie made his way to New York City in search of a band to join. His first job was with Cab Calloway's orchestra. It lasted until 1941, when Calloway allegedly fired the young trumpeter after growing tired of all his pranks.

Gillespie then played with a number of different bandleaders. He also began experimenting at all-night jam sessions with several other young musicians, including Charlie "Bird" Parker, Thelonious Monk, Max Roach, J.J. Johnson, Clark Terry, Bud Powell, and Milt Jackson. Bebop —a term Gillespie is credited with inventing—grew out of these sessions. With its complex new rhythms and sounds, it was very much unlike the then-popular swing and big band dance music, and it launched a revolution in modern jazz. Later, Gillespie almost singlehandedly invented Afro-Cuban jazz by blending Latin rhythms with mainstream jazz.

Gillespie toured extensively during the 1960s, 1970s, and 1980s, giving as many as 300 shows per year until he became too ill to perform. He also made more than 500 recordings during his lifetime. Among his biggest hits were "Salt Peanuts" (a popular novelty song from the 1940s), "Manteca," "A Night in Tunisia," "Groovin' High," "Con Alma," and "Woody 'n' You." He won nearly every imaginable musical prize, too, including a special Grammy legend award and a National Medal of Arts award in 1989 and Kennedy Center honors in 1990.

January 18. For the first time since Martin Luther King Day became an official federal holiday, all fifty states marked its observance, even longtime holdouts New Hampshire and Arizona. (Also see entries dated November 2, 1983; January 18, 1988; November 6, 1990; and January, 1992.)

January 19. Reginald Lewis, the chairman of TLC Beatrice International, the nation's largest black-owned business, died of a cerebral hemorrhage in New York City. The fifty-year-old executive had been diagnosed with brain cancer about two months earlier.

Lewis's background in Baltimore, Maryland, was a modest one. He left there to earn a degree in economics from Virginia State University and a law degree from Harvard University in 1968. He then joined a New York City law firm and specialized in corporate and securities (stocks and bonds) law.

331

In 1973, Lewis established his own law firm. Ten years later, he set up an investment company, TLC Group L.P. Its first big deal was to buy the McCall Pattern Company, which produces sewing patterns. In 1987, Lewis went after the multi-national food distribution company Beatrice for $985 million. It was the largest deal of its kind in history.

Despite his status as the country's most prominent black businessman, Lewis always downplayed the importance of race in his career. He preferred to be judged by his performance, and he refused to consider race as a crutch or an obstacle. "It's understandable that [my race] is something people focus on," he once remarked. "But what I focus on and what others focus on are two different things.... I focus on doing a first-rate job on a consistent basis."

Lewis's success eventually brought him a personal fortune of some $400 million. Although he carefully guarded his own and his family's privacy, he was well known for his generous donations to civic and charitable causes, including a $1 million gift to Howard University and a $3 million gift to Harvard Law School. (See entry dated November, 1992.)

January 20. At President Bill Clinton's inauguration, renowned black poet Maya Angelou read the special verse she had been asked to compose for the occasion. (She was the first poet asked to participate in the festivities since Robert Frost was part of John F. Kennedy's inauguration in 1961.) Entitled "On the Pulse of Morning," her poem reflected the optimism many people felt at the thought of the country's "new beginnings" under a different administration.

Born Marguerite Johnson in 1928 in St. Louis, Missouri, Angelou grew up there as well as in a small Arkansas town where she was sent to live with her grandmother after her parents divorced. Raped by her mother's boyfriend when she was eight, she then withdrew into a silent world of anger, confusion, and guilt for five years.

Reading and writing poetry slowly helped bring Angelou out of her shell, as did the encouragement of her grandmother and another older woman who became her friend. As a teenager, she left Arkansas to live with her mother in San Francisco, California. There she became the city's first female streetcar conductor. She also gave birth to a son at the age of sixteen. A strong desire to be as independent as possible led her to work at many different jobs to support the two of them.

During the 1950s, Angelou enjoyed success as a dancer, singer, and actress, mostly in New York City. She even toured Europe and Africa in a production of the play

Maya Angelou

Porgy and Bess. After returning to the United States, she resumed her career as a night-club performer and also became active in the civil rights movement as a coordinator for the Southern Christian Leadership Conference (SCLC). Angelou then moved to Cairo, Egypt, in 1961, where she served as an editor on the staff of an English-language newspaper. From there she went to Accra, Ghana, and continued to work in journalism as well as teach.

Angelou came back to the United States in 1966 and began acting again. She also devoted herself to a number of writing projects, including songs, a television series on African influences in American life, and screenplays. But by far her most famous work is *I Know Why the Caged Bird Sings,* the story of her life up until the age of sixteen. Published in 1970, it met with tremendous critical and popular success for its honest and moving look at a young girl's life in the rural South.

Angelou has since produced four more volumes of autobiography, *Gather Together in My Name* (1974), *Singin' and Swingin'* and *Gettin' Merry Like Christmas* (1976), *The Heart of a Woman* (1981), and *All God's Children Need Traveling Shoes* (1986). She has also published several volumes of poetry, including *Just Give Me a Cool Drink of Water 'fore I Diiie* (1971) and *I Shall Not Be Moved* (1990).

Besides writing, Angelou has continued to act and even received an Emmy nomination in 1977 for her performance in the television miniseries *Roots*. Since the 1970s, she has also taught at a number of universities across the United States. In 1981, Angelou accepted a lifetime appointment as professor at Wake Forest University in North Carolina.

January 24. Just days after illness forced him to cancel plans to swear in new Vice-President Al Gore, retired Supreme Court Justice Thurgood Marshall died of a heart attack in Bethesda, Maryland. An outspoken opponent of the conservative direction the country had taken since 1980, the eighty-four-year-old jurist had once vowed that he would not die until the Democrats were in the White House again.

On the Wednesday after Marshall's death, nearly 20,000 people filed past his coffin in the Great Hall of the Supreme Court. There they paid their respects to the man known as "Mr. Civil Rights" in recognition of his lifelong commitment to achieving justice for all, especially the poor and minorities. The next day, 4,000 civil rights leaders, members of Congress, and others (including the president and the vice-president and their wives) gathered at Washington's National Cathedral for a memorial service. Marshall was buried on Friday at a private ceremony at Arlington National Cemetery. (Also see entries dated May 17, 1954; September 23, 1961; July 13, 1965; June 13, 1967; and June 27, 1991.)

January 25. Bert Andrews, a photographer whose work chronicled the history of black theater, died of cancer in New York City. He was sixty-three.

Andrews photographed many of Broadway's biggest stars, including James Earl Jones, Cicely Tyson, Denzel Washington, Billy Dee Williams, Lou Gossett, Jr., Morgan Freeman, Phylicia Rashad, Raymond St. Jacques, and Diana Sands. He also took pictures of memorable scenes from the shows *Ma Rainey's Black Bottom, A Soldier's Play,* and *Bubbling Brown Sugar,* to name a few. Much of his work is on display at the Schomburg Center for Research in Black Culture in Harlem, New York, and in the 1990 book *In the Shadow of the Great White Way: Images from the Black Theater.*

January 26. After nearly two years of negotiations, a spokesman for the U.S. Justice Department announced that an agreement had been reached in a racial discrimination dispute between the Federal Bureau of Investigation (FBI) and its black agents.

Under the terms of the agreement, more than 100 black special agents were scheduled for promotions, transfers, or new training that had been denied to them as a result of racial bias in the overwhelmingly white federal agency. (At the time of the settlement, about 90 percent of FBI agents were white males; only about 5 percent were black.) The FBI also agreed to let a federal judge supervise its personnel practices for five years. In addition, the agency planned to hire outside consultants to study its procedures for promoting, evaluating, and disciplining special agents, and it pledged to change the way in which it chooses agents for assignments and training programs.

White agents opposed to the settlement later took steps to challenge it in federal court. They felt it was a "race conscious" agreement that violated the equal employee rights of non-black agents.

January 30. Thomas A. Dorsey, "the father of gospel music," died of Alzheimer's disease at his home in Chicago, Illinois. He was ninety-three.

Born in Georgia in 1899, Dorsey grew up in a very religious household as the son of a Baptist preacher. By the age of twelve, however, he was playing the piano professionally in bars and bordellos, specializing in the blues and ragtime. He then moved on to vaudeville, where he was known as "Georgia Tom" when he toured with stars such as Ma Rainey and Trixie Smith. In partnership with guitarist Tampa Red, Dorsey also wrote and performed a steady stream of suggestive blues tunes during the 1920s, including the million-seller "It's Tight Like That."

But during the same decade, the death of a friend and his own illness as well as a need to find a balance between his Christian upbringing and his love of the blues led Dorsey to begin experimenting with religious music, too. In 1926, he composed his first piece, "If You See My Savior, Tell Him That You Saw Me." It did not become a hit until it was sung at the National AME Baptist Convention in 1930. (Later, Mahalia Jackson recorded a version that was very popular.) Even then, it took a while for Dorsey's energetic blend of blues, ragtime, and religious music, which he called "gospel," to be accepted by churches. Many people felt it was scandalous and would have nothing to do with it. But it reached audiences in ways that even the greatest preachers couldn't.

By the early 1930s, Dorsey had turned to writing only gospel music. He produced about 1,000 songs over his long career. Among the most famous are "Sweet Bye and Bye," "Peace in the Valley," "Take My Hand, Precious Lord," and "We Shall Walk through the Valley in Peace." They later influenced black singers from James Cleveland and Aretha Franklin to Edwin Hawkins and the Winans. Some even became very popular with white southerners when they were recorded by singers such as country star Red Foley and rock and roll's Elvis Presley.

January. In Fulton County, Georgia, Jackie Barrett was sworn in as the nation's first black female sheriff.

January. In Alabama, black legislators celebrated a courtroom victory that ended

Governor Guy Hunt's practice of flying a Confederate flag over the state capitol in Montgomery. According to a circuit court judge, an 1895 law says that the only acceptable flags are the U.S. flag and the state flag.

The legislators had decided to take the issue to court because they felt the Confederate flag is an offensive symbol of racial oppression and hatred. Various Alabama business groups agreed and spoke out against the governor, too, insisting that displaying the rebel banner hurt the state's image. (Also see entries dated January 31, 1988, and December 12, 1992.)

February 3. Major League Baseball owners fined Cincinnati Reds owner Marge Schott $25,000 and suspended her from the game for one year for her alleged use of racial slurs. (See entries dated November 24, 1992, and December 7, 1992.)

Under the terms of the suspension, Schott was banned from watching games in the owner's box. She was also forbidden from running the team's day-to-day business but was allowed to be involved in major decisions. Her fellow owners also agreed to cut her suspension to only eight months if she behaved herself and if she attended a multicultural training program.

Many people, including Atlanta Braves vice-president Henry "Hank" Aaron, were dissatisfied with this punishment. They felt it amounted to little more than a slap on the wrist for Schott. They had hoped that the other team owners would remove her from the game completely and permanently.

February 6. Tennis great Arthur Ashe, the only black man to win the Wimbledon championship, died of AIDS-related pneumonia in New York City. He was forty-nine.

Ashe had shocked the sports world in April, 1992, when he confirmed rumors that he had contracted the fatal disease as a result of open-heart surgery during the early 1980s. (See entry dated April 7, 1992.) He had kept his condition secret since learning about it in 1988 in order to protect his family and allow them to live as normal a life as possible.

Although he had been ill on and off for several months before his death, Ashe had kept up a busy schedule of speeches, protests, and personal appearances on behalf of various causes, including the anti-apartheid movement, racism in sports, the U.S. government's policy toward Haitian refugees, and AIDS research. He also contin-ued to discuss many of the same topics in articles he wrote for newspapers and magazines. In addition, Ashe set up and helped raise funds for the Arthur Ashe Foundation for the Defeat of AIDS. (Also see entry dated July 5, 1975.)

February 6. In New York City, heavyweight boxing champion Riddick Bowe retained his title by taking only a little more than two minutes to defeat challenger Michael Dokes.

February 23. The city of New York voted to make an eighteenth-century African American burial ground in Manhattan a historical landmark.

The site was first discovered in 1991 during construction of a federal office building. Scientists were eventually called in, and they eventually took away the remains of over 400 people and thousands of artifacts for closer inspection. Most of the blacks who had been buried there were believed to have died between 1710 and 1790.

In September, 1993, the skeletal remains of the African Americans were turned over to anthropologists at Howard University for further study. Once they have completed their work — which is not expected to be until 1999 — the remains are scheduled to be returned to New York City and reburied. Plans are also under way for an African Burial Ground Museum and Research Center to be built near the site of the historic discovery.

February 24. At Grammy Award ceremonies in Los Angeles, California, pioneer rocker "Little" Richard Penniman and the late jazz greats Fats Waller and Thelonious Monk were among the recipients of Lifetime Achievement Awards. Other big winners included Michael Jackson, who took home a Grammy Legends Award, and the group Arrested Development, which was named best new group and best rap group. Made up of members ranging in age from eighteen to sixty-one, Arrested Development won praise for its unique brand of thoughtful, sensitive rap that encourages spiritual questioning and growth.

February 25. In Los Angeles, California, opening arguments began in the federal trial of four white police officers charged with beating black motorist Rodney King.

In this second trial, Stacey Koon, Theodore Briseno, Laurence Powell, and Timothy Wind faced charges of violating King's civil rights. Their first trial on criminal charges related to the same incident ended with acquittals on all but one charge. The verdicts triggered days of deadly rioting in Los Angeles and elsewhere throughout the country. (See entries dated March 14, 1991; April 4-8, 1991; July 9, 1991; April 29-May 1, 1992; May 2, 1992; and October 22, 1992.)

The central issue in the federal case revolved around whether the officers had used excessive force and whether they intended to punish King. (If convicted, they faced up to $250,000 in fines and ten years in prison.) The federal trial was expected to follow along the same lines as the criminal trial with one difference—Rodney King himself was scheduled to take the stand for the first time and testify about his beating. (Also see entry dated April 17, 1993.)

March 8. Singer Billy Eckstine, popularly known as "Mr. B.," died in Pittsburgh, Pennsylvania, at the age of seventy-eight. During the late 1940s and early 1950s, his rich baritone voice made him one of America's top vocalists and among the first to become a crossover star with white audiences. With his coolly casual look—a shirt with a rolled collar and a jacket loosely draped from his shoulders—Eckstine was also pop music's first black male sex symbol.

Born William Clarence Eckstein in Pittsburgh in 1914, he grew up in Washington, D.C., and attended Howard University. He started singing when he was about seven and drifted into it professionally during the 1930s. His first performances were with various amateur shows and dance bands that toured throughout the East and Midwest.

In 1939, Eckstine joined Earl "Fatha" Hines's orchestra and taught himself to play the trombone and trumpet. But it was as a singer that he helped the band gain national fame with two hit records, "Jelly, Jelly" and "Stormy Monday Blues." Eckstine left Hines in 1943 and spent a year as a solo act before pulling together his own band. It did much to popularize the new bebop style of jazz by featuring some of its greatest performers, including Miles Davis, Dizzy Gillespie, Charlie "Bird" Parker, Sarah Vaughan, Dexter Gordon, and Art Blakey.

During the late 1940s, Eckstine turned once again to a solo singing career. He then sang one hit romantic ballad after another. Among his biggest successes were "Fools Rush In," "Everything I Have Is Yours," "Prisoner of Love," "My Foolish Heart," "Body and Soul," "I Apologize," "Blue Moon," and "Passing Strangers." By singing such love songs when a white woman might be listening, Eckstine challenged one of the biggest taboos of a segregated society. "We weren't supposed to sing about love," he later recalled. "We were supposed to sing about work or blues."

Despite his popularity, Eckstine was rarely offered opportunities to work in movies or on television on account of his race. And when he did make an appearance, he was told not to let his eyes rest on any of the white actresses watching him sing. So he spent the rest of his career entertaining enthusiastic audiences in major jazz clubs across the country.

March 23. In Fort Worth, Texas, an all-white jury sentenced an admitted white supremacist to ten years' probation for the June, 1991, drive-by shooting of a black man, Donald Thomas. Thomas was sitting in his pickup truck talking with some white neighbors when he was killed by shots fired from a car in which an eighteen-year-old white skinhead named Christopher W. Brosky was riding.

During Brosky's trial, it was revealed that he had helped plan the shotgun slaying of the thirty-two-year-old Thomas. Two seventeen-year-olds who were also involved, including the alleged triggerman, pleaded guilty and received prison terms. Brosky himself could have received life in prison for his part in the crime. But according to some jurors, his exceptionally light sentence came about as a result of a poorly worded note to the judge. What they had meant to recommend was that he serve five years in jail and then be put on probation for ten years. Instead, what they wrote was interpreted to mean only ten years' probation and no jail time.

The decision infuriated local blacks and sent thousands into the streets on March 28 to participate in what they called a "silent death march." A crowd estimated at more than 5,000 people assembled in downtown Fort Worth and walked peacefully to the county courthouse, where they held a rally calling for justice for African American victims of crime.

March. Astronaut Mae Jemison, the first black woman in space, resigned from the National Aeronautics and Space Administration (NASA). (See entry dated September 12, 1992.) Her immediate career plans included teaching at New Hampshire's Dartmouth University and establishing a technology firm in Houston, Texas, to improve communications and health care in western Africa. Later, it was announced that Jemison was also scheduled to appear in an episode of the syndicated television series "Star Trek: The Next Generation."

April 1. The nationwide Denny's restaurant chain announced that it had reached a settlement with the U.S. Justice Department in a case of alleged racial discrimination against black customers.

339

The Justice Department had accused Denny's of treating black customers less favorably than white customers and of discouraging black customers from eating there. Restaurant officials denied the charges, but as part of the chain's settlement with the Justice Department, it agreed to hire a civil rights monitor and train its employees and managers to oppose racial discrimination. The company also pledged to let people know about its non-discrimination policy through advertisements in newspapers and on television and on notices appearing in the restaurants themselves.

Still waiting to be settled, however, was a lawsuit against the chain filed by an ex-employee claiming racial discrimination. And in March, 1993, some black customers in California had filed a class-action lawsuit against Denny's. They charged that restaurant managers often refused to serve blacks and threatened them or threw them out. They also said they were routinely the target of racial slurs and insults. Finally, they claimed that managers required them to prepay for their meals or pay a cover charge, and that Denny's would not extend the chain's free birthday meal offer to them. (Also see entry dated May 24, 1993.)

April 4. Across the United States, thousands of people observed the twenty-fifth anniversary of the death of Martin Luther King, Jr., with speeches, rallies, and other events. Memorial services were also held in Atlanta, Georgia, and Memphis, Tennessee.

April 6. In a surprise, come-from-behind victory over a better-known opponent who also happened to be his former high school counselor, Freeman Bosley, Jr., won election as the first black mayor of St. Louis, Missouri. A thirty-eight-year-old lawyer, he had been serving as clerk of the circuit courts for the past eleven years.

April 8. Singer Marian Anderson, whose 1939 concert at Washington, D.C.'s Lincoln Memorial was a symbolic triumph over racial bigotry, died in Portland, Oregon, of complications from a stroke. She was ninety-six.

Anderson had first become a national hero of the civil rights struggle after the Daughters of the American Revolution (DAR) refused to allow her to perform at their hall in the nation's capital on account of her race. Instead, she gave a stirring concert on Easter Sunday, 1939, that attracted a spellbound, racially mixed audience of some 75,000 people.

Anderson continued her quiet struggle for racial dignity and equality throughout the remainder of her life. Besides putting to rest the idea that blacks could not excel in the world of opera and classical music, she devoted her time, talent, and money to a variety of causes. In 1958, for example, she was named a U.S. delegate to the United Nations. In this position, she served on a committee that watched over colonies in Africa and the Pacific Ocean area that were in the process of becoming independent countries. She also contributed generously to the NAACP, the Urban League, the YMCA, the International Committee on African Affairs, and the Freedom from Hunger Foundation.

In 1963, Anderson received the Medal of Freedom (the U.S. government's highest civilian honor) for her outstanding contributions to the ideals of freedom and democracy. She retired from performing in 1965. As she once wrote in her autobiography, *My Lord, What a Morning,* "My mission is to leave behind me the kind of impression that will make it easier for those who follow." (Also see entries dated March, 1939, and January 7, 1955.)

April 9. After a year-long search, the NAACP board of directors announced that they had chosen forty-five-year-old clergyman and activist Ben Chavis to replace Benjamin Hooks as executive director of the nation's oldest civil rights group.

The energetic and progressive Chavis came to the NAACP from Cleveland, Ohio. He had worked there for the United Church of Christ's Commission for Racial Justice for twenty-five years, the last eight as its executive director. Originally from North Carolina, he received a bachelor's degree from the University of North Carolina, a master of divinity degree from Duke University, and a doctorate degree from Howard University.

A civil rights activist since joining the NAACP at the age of twelve, Chavis spent four years in prison during the late 1970s as a member of the so-called Wilmington Ten. This was a group of nine black men and one white woman who were convicted of firebombing a white-owned store in Wilmington, North Carolina, during a period of unrest over school desegregation. Chavis and the others had, in fact, been in town to protest but denied taking part in any bombing. The controversial case prompted Amnesty International to declare the Wilmington Ten political prisoners, making them the first people to be identified as such in the United States. A federal appeals court eventually overturned the convictions after witnesses admitted they had lied while giving testimony.

Later, Chavis made a name for himself as one of the founders of the "environmental racism" movement. This group claims that unusually high amounts of toxic materials are stored in and near black communities.

As the new head of the NAACP, Chavis pledged to make the organization more aggressive and more in tune with young blacks and blacks in the inner cities. Describing himself as a Pan-Africanist, he also reached out to Africans all over the world by announcing plans to set up NAACP branches in Africa and the Caribbean. In addition, he promised to expand the membership of the NAACP to include other minorities.

April 9. In Memphis, Tennessee, U.S. Representative Harold Ford—the state's first black member of Congress—was acquitted of charges that he accepted over $1 million in bank loans he never intended to repay from people seeking political favors from him. His first trial on the same charges ended in a mistrial in 1990. (See entry dated April 27, 1990.)

April 11. Janet Harmon Bragg, the first black woman in the United States to earn a full commercial pilot's license, died at the age of eighty-six in a suburb of Chicago, Illinois.

A native of Georgia, Bragg graduated from Spelman College and did graduate work at Loyola University and the University of Chicago. She developed her interest in flying in 1930 while she was dating one of the country's first black flight instructors. She then took flying lessons and in 1933 bought the first of three airplanes she eventually owned.

Two years later, Bragg was one of the first nine blacks admitted to the Curtiss Wright Aeronautical University to study aircraft mechanics. After being denied the opportunity to try out for her commercial pilot's license in Alabama on account of her race, she headed north to Illinois, where she was able to take and pass the test.

Bragg later formed the black Challenger Air Pilots Association and helped train Ethiopian soldiers during World War II. She continued to fly as a hobby throughout the 1950s, 1960s, and 1970s.

April 12. Central Michigan University basketball coach Keith Dambrot, who is white, was fired from his job for using a racial slur in front of his team when referring to his black assistant coach.

At a team meeting during the season, Dambrot allegedly told his fifteen players—twelve of whom were black—that he wished "we had more niggers on this team." He later explained that he hadn't meant he needed more black players, just tougher team play in the midst of a losing season.

Some of the black members of the team defended their coach. They said they were not offended by what he had said and that he was not a racist. They insisted that his use of the word "nigger" had been misunderstood by outsiders. "If this were a black coach saying that, nothing would have been made of it," declared one. "It's just one of those things that's getting blown out of proportion."

April 14. A spokeswoman for Attorney General Janet Reno confirmed that she had ordered the civil rights division of the U.S. Justice Department to look into a series of suspicious hanging deaths in Mississippi jails.

For nearly a year, civil rights activists had been calling for an investigation into the deaths of twenty-four black men over a six-year period. All had died by hanging while in police custody in various county jails. During the same period, twenty-three white prisoners had also been found hanged. Authorities ruled that all but one of the forty-seven deaths were suicides. Civil rights activists charged, however, that at least three black prisoners were actually lynched.

April 17. In Los Angeles, California, a federal jury convicted white police officers Stacey Koon and Laurence Powell of violating the civil rights of black motorist Rodney King. Two other officers—Theodore Briseno and Timothy Wind—were acquitted.

While the verdicts in the officers' criminal trial a year earlier had sparked several days of deadly rioting, the verdicts in their federal trial were met with joy and relief. Los Angeles remained calm, as did other cities across the nation. Police and National Guard troops had been on alert for days in anticipation of violence as jurors worked to reach a decision.

On August 4, 1993, a judge handed down his sentences in the case. Both Koon and Powell received thirty months in prison, several years less than most observers had anticipated. The judge explained that he had chosen a lighter punishment because King's behavior had provoked police and because the two officers already had endured the loss of their jobs and a tremendous amount of notoriety. He also speculated that they faced the possibility of abuse in prison.

Blacks reacted to the sentences with anger and disbelief. They felt justice still had not been served in the case.

April 28. President Bill Clinton nominated fifty-five-year-old Lee Brown as head of the U.S. Office of National Drug Control Policy, a cabinet-level position. The person who holds it is often referred to as the "drug czar."

Brown came to the White House with a background in law enforcement. He had formerly served as head of the police departments in Atlanta, Georgia (1978-1982), Houston, Texas (1982-1990), and New York City (1990-1992). He was the first black and the first police officer ever chosen to lead the country's war on drugs.

April 30. In Kansas City, Missouri, the first National Urban Peace and Justice Summit got under way in an inner-city Baptist church.

The unusual three-day meeting was deliberately scheduled to coincide with the first anniversary of the Los Angeles riots. (See entry dated April 29-May 1, 1992.) It brought together over 100 current and former gang members, community organizers, and religious leaders from twenty-six cities across the country. (About half the participants were black, and the other half were Hispanic.) They discussed how to stop the violence in America's urban areas (including ways to expand the gang truce in Los Angeles that began after the riots), fostering neighborhood economic development, dealing with police brutality, and gaining political power.

April 30. President Bill Clinton nominated University of Pennsylvania law professor Lani Guinier as assistant attorney general for civil rights, one of the most important posts in the Justice Department. If confirmed, she would be the first black woman ever to head the civil rights division. (Also see entry dated June 3, 1993.)

May 6. Outside South Boston High School in Massachusetts, racial violence erupted between black and white students.

The problem began earlier in the day when about 100 black and white students walked out of class to protest what they felt were inadequate security measures at the school. Classes ended up being dismissed early on account of the peaceful demonstration. As black students got on buses to ride home, a crowd of white students began throwing rocks and bottles at them. The two groups also exchanged racial slurs, and several people—including Boston's mayor, who had come to the school to talk to the students about security—received minor injuries.

During the mid-1970s, South Boston High School was the scene of the nation's most brutal battles against court-ordered busing to achieve desegregation.

May 6. In a courtroom in Boston, Massachusetts, a jury ruled in favor of Boston University in a long-running dispute between the school and the family of Martin Luther King, Jr., over ownership of about one-third of the slain civil rights leader's personal papers. (See entry dated February 20, 1988.)

On July 16, 1964, King had sent a letter to officials at Boston University (where he had received his doctorate degree) saying that he wanted to give his correspondence, manuscripts, and other papers and items of historical interest to the school's library. Later that year and the next, he did indeed hand over about 83,000 documents. Most dated back before 1961 and covered the birth of the civil rights movement.

In her lawsuit, King's widow, Coretta Scott King, claimed that her husband had changed his mind about the donation before his death but that he had never let the university know. She said that he had only sent his papers up north temporarily because he thought they would be safer there than anywhere in the South. (At the time, his home and office were often the targets of firebombings.) According to Mrs. King, he really intended for them to be returned to him at some future date.

Describing herself and her family as deeply disappointed about the verdict, Coretta Scott King said she would consider filing an appeal. She had hoped to bring all of her husband's papers together in Atlanta, Georgia, at the Martin Luther King Jr. Center for Non-Violent Social Change.

May 11. In Chattanooga, Tennessee, a grand jury decided not to charge any white police officers in the choking death of a black motorist.

The incident occurred on February 5, 1993, when thirty-nine-year-old Larry Powell was pulled over by two police officers who suspected him of driving while drunk. Powell allegedly resisted arrest, and five other officers responded to a call for help from the two officers on the scene. In the scuffle that followed, the officers handcuffed Powell, put him face down on the ground, then gripped his neck with their hands and batons. A medical examiner testified that this choke hold caused

Powell's death but that there was no evidence of abuse.

Outraged black leaders in Chattanooga as well as Powell's widow strongly condemned the grand jury's decision.

May 12. After nearly three years, blacks in Miami, Florida, called off a tourism boycott that had cost the city an estimated $50 million.

The boycott had begun shortly after local government officials snubbed South African anti-apartheid leader Nelson Mandela during his visit in June, 1990. (See entries dated June 20-30, 1990, and October, 1990.) It ended when blacks in the Miami area felt they had finally convinced Hispanic and white business and government leaders to give them more economic and political power.

May 14. In Bronx, New York, the NAACP began organizing its first Hispanic chapter. The move was part of an effort by new executive director Ben Chavis to broaden the group's membership by reaching out to other minorities.

May 16. Singer Marv Johnson, creator with Berry Gordy of the famous Motown sound, died two days after suffering a stroke during a concert in South Carolina. He was fifty-four.

Johnson was the first singer that Gordy recorded and managed. The two of them combined Johnson's background in gospel music with a churchy-sounding female chorus and a male bass to create a uniquely African American product that appealed to black as well as white audiences. The new sound debuted in 1959 with a song entitled "Come to Me" that Johnson recorded on the United Artists label. He had his first big hit a year later with "You Got What It Takes."

Several other hits followed over the next few years, but by the 1970s, Johnson's popularity had begun to decline. He continued to go on tour throughout the United States and Europe, however, often appearing on stage with various Motown superstars.

May 18. In Toledo, Ohio, two members of a white supremacist group called the White Aryan Religion were arrested for planning to blow up a predominantly black public housing project on July 4.

Police said that Aaron Lee and Craig Lay, both twenty-two years old, had plotted to make several bombs and place them around a housing project on the city's east side. During a raid on Lay's house, authorities seized explosives, guns, drugs, and hate literature. They said it appeared that the White Aryan Religion was a new group based in the Toledo area that may have also been responsible for some crimes in nearby Detroit, Michigan.

May 18. Librarian of Congress James Billington named forty-year-old black poet Rita Dove as U.S. poet laureate. She was the first African American woman to serve in the ceremonial post. (Author Gwendolyn Brooks was a consultant on poetry to the Library of Congress before the poet laureate position was created.) The job of U.S. poet laureate—a term borrowed from the British—is to promote poetry through the library's literature programs and advise the library on literary matters.

A native of Akron, Ohio, Dove intended to become a lawyer when she first went off to Miami University of Ohio. But she changed her mind and decided to devote herself to poetry instead. She earned her bachelor's degree at Miami and her master's of fine arts degree at the University of Iowa. Dove then embarked on a teaching career. At the time of her appointment to poet laureate, she was a professor of creative writing at the University of Virginia in Charlottesville.

Dove is the author of four volumes of poetry, many of which focus on people and events in her own family. One of her collections, *Thomas and Beulah,* won the Pulitzer Prize in 1987. She has also written a book of stories, *Fifth Sunday,* a novel, *Through the Ivory Gate,* and a play.

May 18. In New York City, a jury ruled that Leonard Jeffries had been wrongly dismissed from his job as chairman of City College's black studies department for criticizing Jews and whites. It then awarded him $400,000.

Jeffries had sued the college for $25 million for replacing him as department chairman. (He remained a member of the faculty, however.) He claimed school officials were upset about a controversial speech he gave in 1991. In that speech, he declared that Jews and the Mafia had conspired to depict blacks in a negative way in the movies and that Jews had financed the African slave trade. While his remarks created an uproar, they were not the reason for his firing, insisted school officials. They maintained that Jeffries was simply a poor administrator.

The jury sided with Jeffries, saying that his constitutional right to free speech had been violated. After the verdict, he vowed to continue his fight to regain his former job as department chairman.

May 22. In Washington, D.C., heavyweight boxing champion Riddick Bowe retained his title by defeating challenger Jesse Ferguson just seventeen seconds into the second round of their fight.

May 24. The University of Pennsylvania dropped racial harassment charges against a white student who called a group of black women "water buffalo."

The incident occurred near midnight on January 13, 1993. A white student named Eden Jacobowitz was trying to study in his room when he was disturbed by some members of a black sorority who were singing and making other noises outside his dormitory window. He leaned out and shouted, "Shut up, you water buffalo!" The angry women, who said they also heard other racial and sexual slurs but could not tell where they came from, complained to campus police.

They tracked down Jacobowitz, who readily admitted that he had made the "water buffalo" comment. (Born in Israel and educated at a Jewish school, Jacobowitz said the words "water buffalo" had come to his mind because a Hebrew word meaning "water oxen" is used to insult thoughtless and disorderly people.) But he denied saying anything else and insisted that his remark had referred to the funny noises the women were making, not to their race.

University officials disagreed and ordered Jacobowitz to write a letter of apology to the women. They also told him he could be put on dormitory probation and that a note would be added to his student file indicating that he had violated the university's code of conduct on racial harassment. Jacobowitz refused to agree to these terms and instead demanded a hearing before a group of students and faculty.

Before the hearing could be held, however, the charges against him were dismissed when the women withdrew their complaints. They said their case had been undermined because they had never had the chance to tell their side of the story. Jacobowitz, on the other hand, had attracted national media attention with his version of what had happened.

May 24. In the African city of Libreville, Gabon, the second African-African American Summit opened. In attendance were more than 1,000 black Americans (including prominent politicians, civil rights activists, religious leaders, corporate officials, and entertainers) and 3,000 Africans, including twenty heads of state.

Organized by African American human rights activist Leon Sullivan, the summit was intended to establish ties between blacks from all nations. Attendees were also scheduled to discuss ways of promoting economic development and improving health care and farming techniques in Africa.

May 24. A little more than a month after announcing it had reached a settlement with the U.S. Justice Department in a racial discrimination complaint, the Denny's restaurant chain faced still more allegations of bias against blacks.

In Baltimore, Maryland, six black Secret Service agents filed a lawsuit claiming that a Denny's in Annapolis, Maryland, had refused to serve them. They had been in town on April 1 with fifteen other agents preparing for a visit by the president. They stopped at a Denny's for breakfast and placed their orders. When no food was delivered, they ordered again several more times. After about an hour, they left the restaurant without having eaten. According to reports, a group of white agents at a nearby table was served promptly.

Denny's officials insisted the problem was related to poor service, not racial discrimination. They said that they had fired the manager of the Annapolis restaurant for failing to report the agents' complaints. The company later agreed to work with the NAACP to visit Denny's restaurants at random throughout the country to make sure blacks were receiving fair treatment. The company also promised to hire more minorities, and the NAACP said it would help provide sensitivity training.

According to newspaper reports, at least ten other complaints had surfaced in five different states since Denny's had promised to make changes in its operations back in April. (See entry dated April 1, 1993.) In June, the company hired black food executive Norman Hill to serve in the newly created job of vice-president of human resources. His job was to help make sure Denny's anti-discrimination policies were followed at the chain's restaurants throughout the country.

May 28. In Orlando, Florida, a racially-mixed jury acquitted a Miami police officer of manslaughter in the 1989 shooting death of a black motorcyclist.

On January 16, 1989, in the predominantly black Overtown section of Miami, Officer William Lozano shot and killed black motorcyclist Clement Lloyd. Lloyd

349

then crashed, fatally injuring his passenger, Allan Blanchard. Lozano claimed the speeding motorcycle had tried to run him over and that he had fired his gun in self defense. The incident touched off three nights of racial violence in Overtown.

In December, 1989, Lozano was convicted of manslaughter in both deaths and sentenced to seven years in prison. In 1991, however, an appeals court ordered a new trial for the policeman on the grounds that the Miami jury had been pressured into finding him guilty because of the threat of more racial violence.

Lozano's 1993 trial was held in Orlando, where authorities hoped it would be easier to find an impartial jury. They also hoped to avoid triggering another riot if he were acquitted.

In the hours after the verdict was announced, Miami remained relatively calm. Police reported only scattered instances of looting and rock- and bottle-throwing in two mostly black neighborhoods. However, outraged community leaders called on the U.S. Justice Department to file civil rights charges against Lozano, but experts considered that unlikely to happen.

May 30. Sun Ra, an influential pianist and orchestra leader who experimented with jazz and many other forms of music, died at the age of seventy-nine. He had been ill since January, 1993, after suffering a series of strokes.

Ra was born Herman Blount in Birmingham, Alabama, in 1914, but he later liked to claim he was born on the planet Saturn about 5,000 years ago. As Sonny Blount, he played in Fletcher Henderson's jazz orchestra during the mid-1940s and also was active in experimental music circles in Chicago, Illinois.

Blount was already a well-known musician when he changed his name to Sun Ra during the 1950s. Along with the name change, he created a whole new identity for himself by drawing from the Bible, black spiritualism, science fiction, and Egyptian mythology. (Ra, in fact, was the name of the ancient Egyptian sun god.) Beginning in 1956, Sun Ra traveled with a multimedia group known as Arkestra that included musicians as well as exotically costumed dancers.

Ra's career spanned sixty years. During that time, he recorded more than 200 albums, including *Saturn, Magic City, Savoy,* and *It's after the End of the World.* They encompassed a wide range of sounds and styles, including bop, gospel, blues, and electronic synthesizers.

Ra considered himself to be a bridge between different generations, and in February, 1993, *Rolling Stone* magazine seemed to confirm that judgment when it called him "the missing link between Duke Ellington and Public Enemy." Yet he was not especially well known in his native country (he spent most of his later years in Europe) and never had the recognition and success that many bigger stars enjoyed.

June 1. In Washington, D.C., the Library of Congress officially obtained thousands of compositions, letters, essays, tapes, photographs, and other memorabilia of the late jazz musician Charles Mingus. He thus became the first African American jazz musician to have all his works stored in the library's permanent collection.

Mingus, who was born in 1922, received classical training on the trombone before he turned to the bass as both a performer and a composer. One of the most creative jazz artists of his generation, he experimented with developing many new and different sounds and rhythms. His work blended elements of eighteenth - and nineteenth - century classical pieces, the church music of his youth, and the styles of earlier jazz greats such as Jelly Roll Morton, Duke Ellington, and Charlie "Bird" Parker. The result was a complex and often sad sounding kind of jazz. Mingus also helped take the bass from a background instrument to one that was featured in solos or that carried the main melody.

Mingus typically used to compose at a piano without writing down a single note. He then had his musicians memorize what he had just composed. He was also famous for rewriting his music again and again, changing and improvising a piece each time he played it. Later in his life, when he was nearly paralysed from Lou Gehrig's disease (a fatal nerve and muscle disorder), he sang his ideas into a tape recorder.

Among his most notable works are "Meditations," which was a hit at the 1964 Monterey Jazz Festival, and "Epitaph," a 2 1/2-hour-long piece for thirty-one musicians that was never performed during Mingus' lifetime. (He died in 1979.) In recent years, however, it has been featured at several concerts and has brought its composer even more acclaim.

June 3. Acknowledging that he did not have enough support in the Senate to win a major confirmation battle, President Bill Clinton withdrew the controversial nomination of Lani Guinier to head the civil rights division of the U.S. Justice Department.

Opposition to the forty-three-year-old law professor had been growing steadily ever since Clinton announced her nomination in late April. Many people—mainly conservative Republicans — charged that her extensive writings about race and politics were too radical and that they seemed to support the idea of racial separatism. They dubbed her the "Quota Queen" because she seemed to call for racial quotas in electing and hiring public officials.

By late May, the White House had begun to hint that perhaps she should pull out of the running. Guinier refused, however, and insisted that her views deserved a fair hearing in the Senate, not just in the newspapers and on television. As the pressure mounted, the president himself announced that he was withdrawing her name from consideration. In announcing his decision, he explained that he had not closely read her writings before choosing her for the civil rights job.

Afterwards, Guinier defended herself by saying that people had misinterpreted her writings. She insisted that she would have never pushed for quotas because of the racial discrimination her father suffered as the only black student at Harvard College in 1929.

Many other people condemned Clinton's move, including members of the Congressional Black Caucus, civil rights organizations, and women's groups. They agreed with Guinier that she had been unfairly judged.

June 7. In Tampa, Florida, pre-trial hearings got under way for two white men accused of kidnapping a black tourist from New York City on New Year's Day and setting him on fire. (See entry dated January 1, 1993.)

Attorneys for Mark Kohut and Charles Rourk immediately asked for the trial to be moved out of town because of extensive local publicity about the case. A third man originally charged in the crime, Jeff Ray Pellett, was scheduled to testify against Kohut and Rourk as part of a plea bargain in which he admitted to helping with an armed carjacking and being an accomplice after a crime.

At first, the judge refused to move the trial out of town. He later changed his mind and moved it across the state to the town of West Palm Beach. Jury selection finally got under way there on August 23, 1993. At the time the trial was scheduled to begin, victim Christopher Wilson was still recovering from the burns he received during the attack.

June 7. In Las Vegas, Nevada, forty-four-year-old heavyweight boxer George

Foreman's comeback attempt ended in defeat as he lost to twenty-four-year-old Tommy Morrison in a twelve-round unanimous decision.

Foreman had originally retired from the ring in 1977 and then began a comeback in 1987. In 1991, he became the oldest fighter ever to challenge for the heavyweight title when he took on Evander Holyfield.

June 8. In Austin, Texas, a nineteen-year-old black teenager named Ronald Ray Howard was found guilty of killing a state trooper in 1992. The case was unusual in that Howard and his attorneys claimed that rap music had driven him to commit the crime and that he should not have to pay for it with his own life. (Since killing the trooper was a capital crime, Howard faced the possibility of receiving a death sentence.)

Howard confessed to the murder but blamed it on years of listening to violent, anti-police "gangsta rap" that made him hate and fear law enforcement authorities. On the night of the incident, he had driven for about 120 miles while the music of California gangsta rapper Tupac Amuru Shakur played. He said he was very angry by the time Trooper Bill Davidson "pulled [him] over for nothing." Actually, Davidson had pulled over Howard because he had a missing headlight.

The power of gangsta rap to influence behavior also promised to be an issue in a related case. Trooper Davidson's widow filed a product liability lawsuit against rapper Shakur and his record company, Time Warner. She charged both of them with contributing to her husband's death.

On July 14, The jury that had convicted Howard decided that the rap music defence was not reason enough to save him from the death penalty. It sentenced him to die by lethal injection for the murder of Trooper Davidson. As one juror observed, "Music can affect people very strongly, I believe, but in the end a person is responsible for their own actions." (Also see entries dated December 26, 1992.)

June 8. A district court judge ordered the U.S. government to release more than 150 Haitian refugees who had been held at an American naval base in Cuba for as long as twenty months after testing positive for the AIDS virus.

Many black Americans had been closely following the problems of the Haitian men, women, and children ever since the Bush administration forbid them from entering the country. Prominent figures such as Jesse Jackson and, before his death, Arthur Ashe, had repeatedly condemned the government's actions as racist and inhumane. They described the crowded and dirty conditions at the naval base where the Haitians lived as little more than an "HIV prison camp." (Also see entry dated June 21, 1993.)

June 8. Scott Barrie, one of the first African American designers to gain fame in the world of fashion, died of brain cancer in Italy. He was fifty-two.

A native of Florida, Barrie—born Nelson Clyde—began creating clothes at the age of ten. He later studied at the Philadelphia Museum College of Art. After working for twenty years in New York City, he moved to Milan, Italy, in 1982. There Barrie worked for the fashion houses of Krizia and then Kinshido. He opened his own showroom in 1988. He specialized in a soft, fluid style of clothing using jerseys and chiffon in designs that appealed mostly to young people.

June 9. Citing personal reasons that were believed to be related to his health, Mayor Maynard Jackson of Atlanta, Georgia, announced he would not seek re-election to a fourth term. (Also see entries dated October 16, 1973, and October 3, 1989.)

June 9. In Minneapolis, Minnesota, twelve African American managers employed by Ford Motor Company in eight different states filed a class-action lawsuit charging racial discrimination in promoting and paying blacks. The suit also claimed that supervisors had used racial slurs in front of several black managers.

The company had no immediate comment other than to say that it has aggressive anti-discrimination policies. The case was not expected to go to trial until 1995.

June 18. In Detroit, Michigan, opening arguments began in the trial of three white police officers charged in the 1992 death of black motorist Malice Green. (See entry dated November 16, 1992.)

According to witnesses who testified for the prosecution, officers Walter Budzyn and Larry Nevers approached Green while he was in his car, which was parked in front of a suspected drug house. They then became angry when he refused to obey their orders to open up his clenched right fist and began beating him with their heavy police flashlights. A third officer, Robert Lessnau, arrived on the scene while the beating was under way. He pulled Green from his car, threw him on the ground, and kicked him. The beating continued until the officers finally allowed a waiting ambulance crew to treat to Green, who died on the way to the hospital. An autopsy later showed he had received at least fourteen blows to the head.

Budzyn and Nevers were charged with second-degree murder in Green's death, and Lessnau faced charges of assault with intent to do great bodily harm. All three men had been fired from the police force after being charged.

Attorneys for the former officers based their defense on doubts about the true cause of Green's death. They did not deny that the policemen had beaten the black man, but they depicted Green as high on drugs and ready for a fight when the officers approached him. The defense attorneys claimed that he had alcohol and cocaine in his system when he died and that he had a diseased heart. They argued that those conditions played a bigger role in his death than the beating did.

On August 23, 1993, two separate juries found former officers Budzyn and Nevers guilty of second-degree murder. They both faced up to life in prison but were allowed to go free on bond while waiting to be sentenced. Meanwhile, their attorneys vowed to appeal the convictions. Former officer Lessnau, who had allowed the judge rather than a jury to decide his case, was found not guilty of assault.

Most black Detroiters praised the verdicts but were angry that Budzyn and Nevers would remain free until their sentencing on October 12.

June 19. James Parsons, who became the country's first black federal judge when President John F. Kennedy appointed him in 1961, died in Chicago, Illinois, at the age of eighty-one.

A native of Kansas City, Missouri, Parsons worked as a teacher during the 1930s and 1940s before earning his law degree at the University of Chicago in 1949. He then taught briefly at John Marshal Law School and was a lawyer for the city of Chicago. From 1951 until 1960, Parsons was an assistant U.S. attorney. He served with the old Superior Court of Cook County (Illinois) for a year before taking the federal judgeship. He remained in the position and was active in trial work until 1992, when he retired due to illness. (Also see entry dated August 9, 1961.)

June 20. President Bill Clinton appointed track star Florence Griffith Joyner co-chair of the President's Council on Fitness and Sports. She was scheduled to share

Florence Griffith Joyner

the job with former basketball player and congressman Tom McMillen. Together, they replaced bodybuilder and actor Arnold Schwarzenegger, who had been appointed by President George Bush.

Griffith Joyner was a standout at the 1988 U.S. Olympic Trials, where she set a world record in the 100 meters. Later that year at the actual Olympic Games in Seoul, South Korea, she won three gold medals and set a world record in the 200 meters.

June 21. The U.S. Supreme Court upheld the Clinton administration's policy of intercepting Haitian refugees in international waters and returning them to their homeland without hearing their requests for political asylum.

The Bush administration had begun the policy in May, 1992, and during the presidential election campaign that year, Bill Clinton had condemned the action as "cruel" and "illegal." But as the country's new chief executive, he backed away from that position and chose instead to follow Bush's lead. Clinton explained that he thought it was the best way to discourage Haitians from making the dangerous boat journey into U.S. waters.

Haitian Americans and others protested the ruling as discriminatory. "It's a Haitians-only policy," declared Harold Koh, a Yale Law School professor who had argued the case in front of the Supreme Court. "It's in nobody's interest to speak for the Haitians, and if you harm the Haitians nobody has to pay except for the Haitians themselves."

June 22. In Detroit, Michigan, the U.S. Post Office unveiled a stamp honoring the late African American boxer Joe Louis on the fifty-fifth anniversary of his stunning defeat over Germany's Max Schmeling. Louis was the first fighter ever to be honored with a stamp. (Also see entries dated June 25, 1935; June 22, 1938; and April 12, 1981.)

June 24. Saying he lacked the energy to continue leading the city, the longtime mayor of Detroit, Michigan, seventy-five-year-old Coleman Young, announced that he would not seek re-election to a fifth term. He had served as mayor since 1973.

June 24. Virginia's L. Douglas Wilder, the country's first black elected governor, revealed that he intended to challenge fellow Democrat Charles Robb for Robb's seat in the U.S. Senate in the 1994 elections. (Also see entries dated November 7, 1989, and September, 1991.)

June 25. The U.S. Supreme Court ruled in a case involving job discrimination that workers do not automatically win bias suits by proving that their employers gave false reasons for firing them. According to legal experts, the new ruling meant that workers who suspected they were fired because of racial discrimination must *prove* the cause of the firing was really rooted in racial bias and not just the result of personal conflicts or other reasons.

June 26. Former Brooklyn Dodgers catcher Roy "Campy" Campanella, who spent the last thirty-five years of his life in a wheelchair following a car accident that ended his career, died in Los Angeles, California, of a heart attack. He was seventy-one.

A native of Philadelphia, Pennsylvania, Campanella was born in 1921 to a black mother and a father of Italian descent. He began playing professional baseball at the age of fifteen and joined the Negro Leagues as a member of the Elite Giants out of Baltimore, Maryland. He became a Dodger in 1948, the year after Jackie Robinson broke the color barrier in major league baseball. (Twenty-one years later, he followed Robinson again, this time as the second black player elected to the Hall of Fame.)

Campanella spent the next ten years as a Dodger. A powerful hitter with exceptional fielding skills and a natural ability to lead, he quickly became one of the game's best all-around catchers. He picked up Most Valuable Player awards in 1951, 1953, and 1955 and was a major force behind the Dodgers' success during the 1950s, which included five pennants and, in 1955, a World Series victory. Always friendly and cheerful, he was also one of the game's most popular stars.

Campanella's dazzling career was cut short one icy night in 1958 when his car skidded off a road on Long Island, New York. The vehicle then overturned, leaving him paralyzed from the chest down. On May 7, 1959, a benefit game between the Dodgers and the Yankees was held in the Los Angeles Coliseum to help pay for the costs of his medical care. In attendance were 93,103 fans, and thousands more were turned away. It was—and still is—the largest crowd ever to attend a major league baseball game.

Despite his disability, Campanella remained active with the Dodgers for the rest of his life. In 1977, he began serving as a special instructor of promising young catchers during the spring training season.

June 26. In Detroit, Michigan, thousands of people assembled to commemorate the thirtieth anniversary of a freedom walk led by Martin Luther King, Jr. They celebrated the occasion with another march and a downtown rally calling for a renewed commitment to political activism, economic justice, and closer ties between people of African descent all over the world.

With a new generation of leaders in attendance—including NAACP executive director Ben Chavis and Martin Luther King III—marchers retraced the same route the slain civil rights leader took on June 23, 1963, along with 125,000 of his supporters. At the end of that historic march, King delivered for the first time a version of his famous "I Have a Dream" speech. The rest of the country heard the final version later that same summer in Washington, D.C.

June 28. The U.S. Supreme Court declared that states may be violating white voters' rights by creating congressional districts that appear to be based only on race.

The ruling—which many legal experts called one of the most significant in a decade—cast doubt on key parts of the 1965 Voting Rights Act. This landmark civil rights law made it possible for blacks to gain more seats in the U.S. Congress as well as in state legislatures. It protected minority voters against discrimination and under-representation at the hands of whites who divided up voting districts in such a way that blacks never would be in the majority, a process known as "gerrymandering."

The new Supreme Court decision also cleared the way for white voters to sue states that go to extremes to create voting districts where black and/or Hispanic voters end up in the majority.

June 30. In California, seventy-five-year-old Tom Bradley stepped down from office after serving as mayor of Los Angeles for twenty years. He had decided earlier not to run for re-election in the face of the city's serious financial problems, rising crime rate, and strained race relations.

A liberal black Democrat, Bradley had been in public service for fifty years at the time of his retirement, first as a policeman and later as a councilman and then as mayor. Taking his place in Los Angeles was a conservative white Republican businessman, Richard Riordan.

June. *Menace II Society, a* film directed by twenty-one-year-old African American twin brothers Allen and Albert Hughes, was a surprise hit at theaters with earnings of more than $10 million in less than a month. The Hughes brothers and their critically acclaimed drama about urban violence had been nominated for awards at the 1993 Cannes Film Festival in France.

June. The often mysterious pop star Prince created a stir when he announced that he had changed his name to a sign that combines the symbols for male and female. The sign had served as the title of his most recent album, and it also appeared in his videos, on his clothing and guitar, and various places on stage with him. But since no spoken word exists for the sign and Prince himself did not provide a pronunciation, no one was sure exactly what he wanted to be called.

June. Black actor-comedian Bill Cosby was reported to be working on a second deal to buy the NBC television network. (See entry dated October 28, 1992.) According to some sources, the deal involved several other unnamed Hollywood insiders besides Cosby.

Index

Index

Index